To Terry, Alysen, Daniel and Raphael

My thanks to Sarah Baxter, Sarah Fitzgerald, Paul Travis, Maggie Brown, Merrill Brown and Patricia Bauer, for reading along as I have been writing, and their comments, criticisms and corrections. You made authorship a little less lonely.

This edition first published by Gibson Square in 2025

rights@gibsonsquare.com
www.gibsonsquare.com

The moral right of Jonathan Miller to be identified as the author of this work has been asserted in accordance with the Copyright, Designs and Patents Act 1988.

SHOCK

OF THE

NEWS

CONFESSIONS
OF A TROUBLEMAKE

Jonathan Mi

Th
in

Pa
tai
acc
Car

All
or tr
othe

CONTENTS

'I'M NOT INTERRUPTING YOU --- AM I?'

Murdoch's Magic Mountain

Where to commence my troublemaker elegy? So much trouble to choose from. The memory of one misadventure melds into another. But one of my biggest escapades of all was as a chief mischief maker for Rupert Murdoch, in his time the global bad boy and king of disruptors. So I'll start this story at his house in Los Angeles.

At his mansion named Misty Mountain in the Santa Monica Hills, Rupert Murdoch was having a cocktail party. I am in the garden, admiring the view, sneaking a cigarette, and looking for a flowerpot to conceal the butt. Rupert hated smoking. He once caught me having a ciggie and remonstrated, 'Stop that. We need you alive.' That was him in one of his transiently charming moods, as when he used to phone me, always in search of gossip, and started the call by asking, 'I'm not interrupting you, am I?'

Murdoch's mansion was not on the scale of La Cuesta Encantada, William Randolph Hearst's castle 250 miles north in San Simeon, the model for Xanadu in the film Citizen Kane. Hearst's estate was big and beyond vulgar, with its 165 rooms, imported treasures, three guesthouses and a garden of 127 acres on a bone-dry rock. Misty Mountain was restrained in comparison, and much more liveable. With only 22 rooms, set in a garden of six acres, in Spanish colonial revival style, vast windows, sweeping vistas, it was a billionaire's mansion, but it oozed taste and Hollywood glamour as well as power.

Murdoch buys and sells houses like he trades wives and Misty Mountain was then his favourite, a symbol of his new status in the film industry. The house had been designed by Wallace Neff, architect to Douglas Fairbanks and Charlie Chaplin. Built in 1926 for film director Fred Niblo, who later went broke, it was then bought by Hollywood tycoon Jules Stein, in a bidding war with Cary Grant. Now it was Rupert's. He was the King of the Hill.

Triumphant in Los Angeles, New York and London, his eyes now on China, Murdoch was at the apogee of his power. He had built an empire upon an empire. Its humble beginnings: a daily in South Australia that he had inherited, aged 21. Now, 40 years later, in 1993, he was master of all he surveyed. He was the Charles Foster Kane of the time. I am here because the monarch of media was entertaining his preening myrmidons, of whom, at the time, I was one. We were all dressed in what we imagined to be our best L.A. evening wear. I had rushed out to the swanky shops on Melrose Avenue that afternoon to find something suitable.

Rupert was married to Anna Torv at the time, a woman who can only be described as forgiving, for it certainly wasn't easy being married to Murdoch. A former journalist, she met Rupert at the *Daily Mirror* in Sydney, a paper he'd bought in 1958, an early trophy on his march to world domination. News Corp. executives from around the world were in the throne room—living room being too modest a description—angling for some face time with the monarch. I've never been one for crowds, so I stayed outside. And I'd already had plenty of face time with the boss.

Rupert had convened a technology week on the 20th Century Fox Studio Lot and there were executives present from many divisions across News Corporation. Our conference was supposed to be the forge of the future. We had spent two days listening to invited outside experts pontificating on their inchoate visions of the future. I recall a consultant from McKinsey, spouting forth and splattering slides on the wall. A man from Apple was there, touting a complicated and primitive personal digital assistant called Newton, which went on to become a giant flop, although it ultimately inspired the iPhone.

A movie lot is maybe not the place to take hard decisions about the future. Everything was surreal, a fantasy. I'd wandered onto the sound stage of Hill Street Blues the day before and was amazed at its authenticity, it was exactly like a real police station in New York! Until I brought myself up short because the only notion I had about what a New York police precinct should look like, was from watching Hill Street Blues.

Rupert was the tycoon's tycoon in a world about to become digital. He was bemused. What was about to hit his newspaper and television businesses that bestrode the world? Indeed, the newspaper boys had not even been invited to his tech shindig. Rupert had smashed the Fleet Street unions and ridden the satellite wave to create Sky in its wake. But the potential and consequences of the internet were eluding him.

I was at that time seen as one of the gurus on all things technological and was invited to lunch with Rupert at the studio commissary after the conference. I met him at Building 88, the old executive building. There was no computer on the desk in his office, when I'd stopped by for our date. We walked to lunch where we were attentively served. He was his charming self but didn't seem entirely present. To me it felt like a potential job interview to the empire's future....

2

SHOCK OF THE NEWS

Adieu El Vino—1986

Shortly after joining *The Times,* I was taken by colleagues to the Town of Ramsgate, which is not in the town of Ramsgate but next to the Thames at Wapping Old Stairs leading down to the river in east London.

The Town of Ramsgate public house is where *Times* journalists hung out during the Wapping dispute, while the mob of printers and their friends besieged the gate of Rupert Murdoch's nearby newspaper fortress. The traditional journalists' pub, El Vino on Fleet Street, had been abandoned, colonised by solicitors.

I was getting a crash course in British newspaper lore. I'd just joined the paper, new cannon fodder arrived from America in the battle to free the British newspaper industry from the tyranny of the printers.

Did I know the best dateline ever filed, asked Tim Jones, one of my new colleagues? I was straight off the boat, metaphorically, and confessed ignorance.

There are twin shapely peaks in the Ezulwini Valley of Eswatini in Southern Africa, he told me, known to the locals as Sheba's Breasts. Finding himself in this happy valley, a correspondent for the *Guardian* cabled, 'Between the breasts of Sheba—I like it here.'

Where journalists gather, the banter is to be taken with plenty of scepticism. The Eswatini story is what's known in the trade as too good to check. So I did check and it's true. It was used as a dateline in 1964 by journalist Arthur Hopcraft in a report for The *Guardian*.

This was the end of an era, and the start of a new one. The Fleet Street memorialised by Evelyn Waugh, in his quintessential newspaper novel *Scoop*, was coming to an end. Rupert had ripped out its heart. *The Times* and the *Sunday Times* had been on Gray's Inn Road, not far away, but the *Sun* and the *News of the World* were at News International's Bouverie Street premises in the heart of the newspaper district. With these premises abandoned in the bolt to Wapping, the old Fleet Street entered a death spiral. Goldman Sachs would soon buy both the *Telegraph* building and the Black Lubyanka building of the *Daily Express*. Reuters would leave for an office tower at Canary Wharf, to be replaced by Freshfields lawyers.

Fortunately the siege of Wapping was usually fairly porous, and business at the Town of Ramsgate was brisk as we snuck out for lunch. Keir Starmer, I subsequently learned, was among the volunteer legal advisors protecting the civil rights of the pickets. I imagine him freezing on the Wapping Highway outside the fortress, while we tucked into our pork pies at the Town of Ramsgate. We didn't know it at the time, but our smug complacency was ill advised. The computers that came for the printers would soon come for us. We couldn't even imagine that something called the internet and artificial intelligence would be threatening us all with obsolescence, too.

The Town of Ramsgate is the only pub I know that has a Papal blessing behind the bar, inscribed by the Vatican calligrapher, and attested by the seal of the Pope himself. The Pope supposedly thought he was blessing the actual Town of Ramsgate in Kent, 150 miles away. That was the story, anyway.

If back then it was the dawn of a new era for journalism, these times are ancient history now. Not even the jokes have stood the test of time. Would you be allowed to file such an intro as Hopcroft's to today's *Guardian*? Breasts present the immediate problem. Maybe between the chests of Sheba? It would all be angrily crossed out by a gender-neutral Zoom generation subeditor, working from home. That's if sub-editors (copy editors in America) even exist anymore.

Best to avoid the subject altogether.

Newspapers—the dead-tree press—are irrelevant now, 40 years later, sad to say, as an ink-stained child of the press myself. You rarely see anyone reading a newspaper, even on a train. W.H. Smith has abandoned the high street. Who wants ink all over their hands? I've hardly bought a paper in years. I have my iPhone, more powerful than the computer that sent men to the moon. On its screen the once-glorious mastheads of famous newspapers are rendered in pixels, not print.

Many fewer trees are being felled, at least. Since I got in the game, circulation has collapsed (I'm not solely responsible). The *Sun* sold 3.6 million copies in 1990, maybe sells 1.2 million now. The figures are no longer disclosed. From embarrassment, without doubt. The *Daily Mail* has gone from 2.3 million to less than a million. In the United States, the *Chicago Tribune*, *Los Angeles Times* and *Washington Post* have all lost more than half their circulation. Newspapers are now mainly websites. The print edition is an afterthought. 'Digital first' is the rallying cry.

In 1871 Henry Morton Stanley, commissioned by the *New York Herald*, tracked the missing, presumed lost David Livingston to Ujiji near Lake Tanganyika, in what is now Tanzania. 'Doctor Livingston, I presume,' was the takeaway quote. His discovery was a sensation on a scale no longer conceivable, in our world of 15-minute news cycles and algorithm-driven information streams.

'You provide the pictures and I'll provide the war,' William Randolph Hearst, proprietor of the *New York Journal*, ordered a photographer, at his megalomaniacal peak. The Spanish-American War duly ensued.[1] Hearst became the model for Citizen Kane, the 1941 movie directed by and starring Orson Welles. 'Mr. Carter, if the headline is big enough, it makes the news big enough,' says Kane in the film.

It's the most classic of numerous movies set in the milieu of newspapers, when they mattered.[2]

Lord Northcliffe's *Daily Mail* shaped the development of aviation, and nurtured the industry that would win the Battle of Britain, with his colossal-at-the-time £10,000 prize for Alcock and Brown's transatlantic crossing in a Vickers Vimy bomber, in 1919. (Although they crash-landed in an Irish peatbog and the American Charles Lindbergh, who made the first solo flight in 1927, got the subsequent glory.) He also wasn't shy picking battles, deposing Lloyd George during the height of the Great War.[3] 'News is what somebody somewhere wants to suppress; all the rest is advertising,' he said.

The *Daily Mail* was selling a million copies a day at the start of the 1920s and twice that by the end of the decade. 'Never pick a fight with a man who buys ink by the gallon and paper by the ton,' said Mark Twain, an author now cancelled in many schools.

All gone. The cacophony of Remington typewriters in the newsroom has been silenced. Nobody is shouting 'copy' or sending cables at night press rate. The spike has surely been banned by health and safety.

I was in Detroit not long ago, where I once worked, visiting the site of a future inner-city horse-riding centre, Detroit Horse Power, where local activists are aiming to transform a derelict wasteland into an urban equestrian park. It is modelled on the Ebony Horse Club in Brixton, London. It's a project that combines my passion for horses, with my hopes for a revival of Detroit, where I learned so much about journalism.

It's counter-intuitive to go on holiday to Detroit, as I did. But it's instructive. Detroit still has many problems but nearly 50 years after the riots made it a dystopia, the once-great city is showing signs of life. Ford has restored the magnificent Union Station. Woodward Avenue looks smart. The downtown streets are clean. There are restored buildings, and flowers in the centre of the boulevards. Gucci has opened a boutique next to the old police headquarters, my old stomping ground. There are some very good restaurants. My Uber driver was from Lomé, Togo, driving a smart, impeccably clean Suburban SUV of which he was very proud. We spoke French. *Je l'aime ici*, he said. So Detroit is becoming a land of opportunity for some.

Out in the now less-densely populated neighbourhoods of Detroit there are urban farms where destroyed houses have been removed and the land restored. People are growing vegetables and fruit. A lot of the remaining houses are being improved. Braver bourgeois families are returning from the suburbs. There's good coffee. With a respected mayor, Detroit has little of the systemic corruption that plagues rival Chicago. There's a vibe of Brooklyn, Michigan. To live in Detroit is no longer dire, it's cool.

But then I visited the soulless *Detroit Free Press* newsroom decanted to a nothingburger downtown office tower, and it was a different story, of decline and fall.

When I started my career at the *Free Press*, the newsroom was a volcano. Not now. All but two journalists were WFH. They only bother to print the paper three times a week. Otherwise it's just another website, focused largely on the city's sports teams. Look on the *Detroit Free Press* and despair. The city's coming back, the newspaper isn't.

Detroit was an important step on my road to Wapping. It's the city where I got a taste of big-city newspapering while it still existed, a city that was then on its knees after riots, depopulation and deindustrialisation, a wonderful city to be a journalist. But the *Detroit Free Press*, the beloved, pesky, unpredictable *Free Press*, is a shadow of its former self, rotting away to irrelevance under the dead hand of its current owner, the Gannett Company.

I will insult Gannett frequently in this book, because it deserves it, and also as a proxy for the awful corporate media groups that have presided over the decline of newspapers in the United States and United Kingdom. It's a decline entirely attributable to the failure of newspaper publishers to stake out their place in a future in which people no longer read newspapers on the train, but watch TikTok videos on their phones. Newspapers are represented on the internet, it's true. But they are nowhere close to being as influential on the digital platforms as they used to be in print. Their journalism isn't compelling anymore against riotous competition. Some of the best young journalists work elsewhere.

Gannett owned 250 newspapers in America by 2019 and it would be hard on any given day to pick up any one of them and declare it a great read. The newspapers are purely a product, standing for nothing. Its flagship national *USA Today* is the newspaper equivalent of a McDonald's hamburger. A read of last resort in the airport departure lounge. Some of the journalists try, but much reads as if it's written by an especially obtuse robot. Gannett boasts of its 'compelling content, events, experiences and digital marketing business solutions.' At Gannett they hold meetings where they conjure up such gibberish, they don't hold the Front Page.

Gannett's style of squeeze-until-the-pips-squeak media ownership is not just an American problem. In Britain its wholly-owned subsidiary Newsquest controls more than 200 media brands, including 150 local newspapers such as the *Oxford Mail*. Dire is aptly descriptive of most of them. I feel sorry for the young journalists who are condemned to work there. Hopefully they will make their escape.

The death or might-as-well-be death of almost all printed newspapers was inevitable but the carelessness with which newspaper publishers surrendered their position is a disheartening story. Newspaper owners were supremely confident. In the seventies groups merged and consolidated in the supposed interest of efficiency, but shareholder value and bonus options were really the priority of management. The papers may not have been as good as they used to be but the profits were fat.

Then the internet arrived in the eighties and nineties with the newspapers' management hardly noticing, or noticing too late. They finally paid attention when the business started falling apart. They were behind the curve at every step. Classified advertising disappeared to Craigslist and eBay,[4] or to local free sheets that dispensed with journalism altogether.

Newspaper publishers had no strategy or even understanding of the changes occurring around them. Their belated response was manic and confused. Newspapers started giving their content away online, thinking that advertisers would like it. But advertisers were finding other routes to the consumer that were cheaper and less wasteful. Some belatedly put up pay walls; the *New York Times* and the *Financial Times* with great success, many others with poor or indifferent results, there being so many competing distractions online. And some, including the *Sun*, were still floundering between the two in February 2025, making some content free and demanding payment for other material frustrating readers either way.

The great replacement of newspapers by digital news isn't finished. Only a handful of newspaper titles will survive in this crowded, disrupted market. The London *Evening Standard*, long reduced to a free sheet, closed in 2024 (re-emerging as a 'new' entity, the London *Standard*). More than 500 American dailies have closed since I entered the game. Many of those clinging on are now so dire they don't deserve to survive. It's not just newspapers but print generally that has seen sales collapse. My favourite newsagent on Berwick Street in Soho, London, tells me that sales of once-thriving magazines like *Hello!* are down by 50 per cent.

We foresaw none of this at the Town of Ramsgate. We thought we were the future but were instead the last of the Mohicans.

3

THE ART OF TROUBLE

Did I ever use a typewriter? Mother's milk. Upright manuals, bashed to bits.
We typed 'the quick brown fox jumped over the lazy dog' to test that every
letter was working. Cut and paste meant exactly that—1969

I arrived at the University of Michigan in Ann Arbor from London
in the summer of 1969, aged 17, hopelessly naive, admitted despite
the absence of most of the normally required academic qualifications. They waived me in only because my father had just been
appointed a professor at the medical school. He'd had enough of
the NHS, even then. A place for me was a perk of his job.

I was initially reluctant to follow my family to Michigan. But I
was a teenager and confused. I'd been at Bedales, a progressive coed
boarding school in Hampshire, where I was noisy and a terrible
student. I subscribed to the *Economist* on the school rate, hid in the
library, wrote a few pieces for the student chronicle, sneaked off to
the Good Intent public house in Petersfield, where they were not
fussy about age, and tried to stay awake in lessons. I recently wrote
a rude piece about the school for the *Spectator* and suspect I am now
persona non grata there. I wasn't interested in A-levels and didn't get
any.

London at the time was supposedly buzzing, decreed to be
'swinging' by *Time* magazine. It was true that London had a photo-
genic and groovy counter-culture. Jimi Hendrix played the Albert
Hall, the Rolling Stones played a gig in Hyde Park. But *Time*'s story

was what is known in the trade as a confection, bearing only an incidental relationship to the broader truth. Away from Bárbara Hulanicki's hip Biba boutique and the anarchic bazaar of Kensington Market, later demolished, the site now a branch of PC World, England was in fact rotting. This was the tag end of Harold Wilson's Labour government. The winter of discontent, the OPEC oil crisis and IMF bailout soon followed.

It was the height of the Vietnam War and I demonstrated outside the American embassy in Grosvenor Square, immersed myself in silly teenage politics, and hung out with friends at music gigs in grotty clubs in Camden Town. I was very left wing at the time (I got over it, eventually) and ran into Peter Mandelson when he was the commissar behind some demo of the day. He was extremely arch and very bossy. I didn't like him, indeed took against him instantly. We were to meet again much later, in Brighton, in an incident I will explain later, when I provoked him into a spectacular hissy-fit.

It's true there were girls with Union Jack mini skirts on the King's Road in Chelsea, but outside the privileged postcodes London was also a tired city of endless grime. They were still clearing remaining bomb sites. People in Cricklewood were living in prefabs.[5] There's a documentary on YouTube, a tour of North London with the suave actor James Mason,[6] disabusing the Swinging London narrative. He talked to bums, showed us the miserable offerings of the market traders, filmed navvies huddled around their braziers.

Withnail and I,[7] which began in squalid Camden Town, was another accurate portrayal of the zeitgeist. But the narrative was Swinging London. The 'easy listening' song England Swings[8] by Roger Miller, was a hit in 1965 in both Britain and the US, and I knew it wasn't true.

None of what was happening in London suggested I could make a living there. University would have been the alternative but I had no qualifications, having become perfectly alienated from school. My economic prospects in Britain were zero. I thought I wanted to be a journalist but didn't have a clue what I had to do to become one.

So I made the move to America. It was like being promoted to Club Class, from grotty, steerage England. Eventually I got a chance to return to Britain, during the government of Margaret Thatcher, when you didn't have to put your watch back 20 years when you landed at Heathrow. But the move to America was the great escape.

I said goodbye to London friends, all heading to universities, and left Britain. I took the BOAC bus from the Victoria Coach Station and flew firstly to Bermuda to visit a school friend whose family had grown wealthy selling rum on Front Street. Then, via La Guardia, on to Detroit airport and then Ann Arbor where the sky was blue and it was blazing hot.

The young and ambitious state of Michigan had implanted in Ann Arbor a university with the mission of becoming the Athens of the Midwest, and it had succeeded. The University of Michigan, founded in 1817, had become one of the best in the world—still is, 18th in the 2025 reputation ranking of *The Times Higher Education Supplement*. President Kennedy launched the Peace Corps from the steps of the Michigan Union.

The university was especially strong in engineering, medicine, science and literature, profited from a generous alumni and boasted the nation's best college football team. Also, and this was my personal nirvana, there was the *Michigan Daily* student newspaper. Here is where I transformed from a directionless exile, vaguely but inconclusively drawn towards journalism, into a cadet journalist. It was like winning the lottery.

Ann Arbor, known by the locals as 'A2,' was nothing like grimy London. It was a shady, prosperous bubble in Midwestern America, the enormous university and its hospital at the centre, surrounded by concentric circles of student housing, the smarter neighbourhoods where the professors lived, and the ranches on the outskirts, petering out to rural Michigan to the north and west, and blending into industrial Ypsilanti, the two big airports to the east, the giant Ford plant where they'd built Liberator Bombers, and then farther still, Detroit and the Canadian border. The University of Michigan dominated the city with 40,000 graduate and undergraduate students.

In its academic cocoon, Ann Arbor was (and still is) one of the most affluent and privileged places on earth but it was also (and still is) a hotbed of extreme politics, ultra-left at the time, now radical identitarian, all about pronouns, Palestinianism and critical race theory.

The year 1969 was the end of the Age of Aquarius, the theme song of the rock musical Hair. The Ann Arbor police had a special radio code—605—as a shorthand description of a hippie. I grew my hair over my shoulders and wore bell-bottom jeans. We must have looked ridiculous.

After London, buses and tubes, Ann Arbor was another world. Kids had cars. They would lend them to you, just like that. Insurance? No problem. Everything seemed enormous, even the food portions in restaurants. The girls were gorgeous. But riot police with shotguns were protecting the administration building.

The horrors of Vietnam and the draft permeated everything. More than 200 American soldiers a week were being killed. Campus politics were passionate and revolutionary and so was the music. Iggy Pop and the MC5 were the town bands in Ann Arbor. The MC5 didn't get a lot of airplay with their hit song, 'Kick Out the Jams, Motherfucker.' The sound was angrier than it had been in London.

Ann Arbor was the birthplace of the radical-left Students for a Democratic Society, which was to morph into the terrorist Weather Underground. Just before I showed up, the local recruiting office of the Central Intelligence Agency had been bombed. It wasn't a huge bomb. Nobody was hurt. It was more of a fuck-you bomb.

The prime suspect was Pun Plamondon, a prominent member of John Sinclair's White Panther Party, although he was never charged. Plamondon died in 2023, Sinclair in 2024,[9] self-exiled in Amsterdam. The White Panther Party used the rainbow flag as its battle standard, not yet a symbol of gay liberation, and campaigned for dope, sex and rock and roll, all abundant in Ann Arbor at the time. It wasn't clear what they would choose, if you offered them two out of three. The White Panther Party no longer exists. Its radicalism has been replaced on American campuses by wokism.

I suppose I never attended more than a couple of dozen lectures in my four years in Ann Arbor and don't recall taking a single exam but many of my professors gave me passing grades anyway and the university never got around to throwing me out. Instead of going to class I immersed myself in the *Daily*. The student newspaper was a pillar of campus life with a reputation as a greenhouse for aspiring journalists. This was the deus ex machina for me. The *Daily* was my miracle. I was lost, then saved. For the next four years, I spent practically every day in its newsroom or out doing stories. Nobody taught me journalism. I learned by doing it.

The *Daily* was owned by the university but written and independently edited by students. It had no connection to the journalism department. It was independent also of the student government, unlike captive student publications in Britain. Nothing resembling at all the American college press has ever existed in Britain. We published six days a week and had news, opinion, arts and sports pages. A student business team sold classified and display advertising. The paper cost a dime and we sold thousands a day. Editors were paid $50 a month.

The newspaper occupied a magnificent Art Deco building near the centre of the campus, designed by Albert Kahn, the architect laureate of Michigan. He was also the architect of the *Detroit Free Press* building, the iconic Fisher Building in downtown Detroit and more than 1000 factories. An Associated Press teletype machine clacked away in a corner. There were dilapidated steel desks with battered manual typewriters. We wrote our stories on rough copy paper and then cut and pasted with scissors and glue.

We were certain the *Daily* was the best student newspaper in America if not the world and may have been right. We saw all the others, which came in the mail on exchange, and none had our verve. We were proud that the *Daily* was a constant irritant to the

19

university, which was powerless to curb it, even though it tried.

We had our own composing room and printing press so the *Daily* building had a pervasive smell of newsprint and ink. On the ground floor was a bank of hot-metal linotype machines that produced type a line at a time from molten lead. The printers would assemble page forms out of lead castings which were then used to make the drums for the letterpress printing machine. The newsroom was upstairs and had a great vaulted ceiling. There was a sign over the sports desk announcing Revolutionary Vanguard Elite. There was a nickel Coke machine at the top of the stairs.

I wasn't the editor, I was considered by my colleagues something of a wild child, but by my senior year was head of features. I launched a daily page one news and gossip column, called Today. Its mascot was a squirrel, the signature creature of Ann Arbor. The *Daily* was also where I met Mrs Miller, who had aspirations to be a journalist before she succumbed to the law. When we met she fell off her chair, but the chair was defective like much of the furniture.

I could basically do anything I liked. I took myself to Montreal after the kidnapping of James Cross, a British diplomat and Senior Trade Commissioner, who was abducted on October 5, 1970 by members of the Front de libération du Québec (FLQ). During the 1972 presidential election, I wormed my way onto George McGovern's doomed campaign, travelling on the press bus with gonzo journalist Hunter S. Thompson, who covered the campaign for Rolling Stone under the rubric, 'Fear and Loathing on the Campaign Trail '72.' He seemed to be the only reporter on the bus to burst the balloon. "How low do you have to stoop in this country to be President?" he wrote.

He wasn't at all as he came across in his supercharged pieces. He was mild-mannered and polite, but a tortured soul who ultimately killed himself.[10] The campaign taught me a lot about political journalism, or rather journalists. These campaign journalists were the subject of a funny but excoriating book by Timothy Crouse. 'Pack journalism is not the result of a conspiracy; it is merely the result of the reporters' natural desire to write what everyone else is writing,' he concluded.

What struck me was the media hierarchy. The superstars were R.W. 'Johnny' Apple of the *New York Times* and David Broder of the *Washington Post*. Then came the 'national reporters' from the news magazines and the 'name' newspapers and newsmagazines like *Newsweek*, the *Boston Globe* and *Chicago Tribune*. They were at the front of the campaign bus with the television network journalists. Then came the 'locals' in the middle like the *Milwaukee Journal*, and finally the squirts like me in the back.

I could see how this pack of journalists was driven mad with its self-importance. Everywhere we went there were crowds and police and secret service. The journalists basked in the attention, imagining it was all for them. And they were partly right. A gaggle of journalists descending on a small town in South Dakota is by itself a spectacle. I was thrilled by this, of course. But later I realised that this pack journalism was hackery, an exercise in groupthink. And every time I have seen a press pack since, this is confirmed in the inevitable huddle as the journalists agree the 'lede,' or 'intro.'

The campaign helped me learn that it is more rewarding to hunt alone than in a pack. So I chased stories all over the state. Stole the trash from the administration building to read the papers of the university president. We got a couple of good stories out of it. ('Gentlemen do not read each other's mail,' said Henry Stimson, Herbert Hoover's Secretary of State. Reporters aren't gentlemen. Surely this should be standard tradecraft for a journalist, like reading upside down the papers on the desks of people you interview.) When an eco-gang started vandalising billboards on the side of Michigan highways, the police were baffled. *Daily* photographer Andy Sachs and I found out who was responsible and we did an eyewitness story watching them destroy a notoriously hideous jumbo billboard advertising Christmas decorations.

There was much sexual entanglement[11] among the staff of the *Daily* and subsequently numerous marriages. This was before Aids and young people apparently going off sex altogether. A Venn diagram of who had sex with whom could be reconstructed and I think by now more than 50 years later, most of us would laugh. Our children and grandchildren have no idea what we got up to. There were histrionics and tantrums. We would argue into the night over the front page layout. We did mad things, throwing the paper's support behind the first Ann Arbor hash bash, a celebration of cannabis, which became a campus tradition and continues at the university even now, after 54 years. I don't think we were ever dull.

My contemporaries at the *Michigan Daily* went on to great things. Eugene Robinson became a columnist for the *Washington Post* and won a Pulitzer Prize. Fred LaBour, whose piece for the paper claiming that Beetle Paul McCartney was dead[12] became a national sensation. He changed his name to Too Slim and became a successful country singer-songwriter. Tony Schwartz went to New York where he was hired by Donald Trump to ghostwrite *The Art of the Deal*. It was a great deal for Tony. Trump offered him half the royalties, which eventually amounted to millions. Patricia Bauer worked as an editor at the White House and then for the *Washington Post*. A near contemporary, Tom Hayden, a former editor and a founder of Students for a Democratic Society, won fame as one of the Chicago Seven, a group of activists charged with conspiracy and inciting a riot at the 1968 Democratic National Convention in Chicago. His conviction was overturned on appeal. Walter Shapiro ran unsuccessfully for Congress[13] before going on to become a Washington political pundit who covered 12 presidential election campaigns before dying just before Donald Trump's victory in 2024. It would have broken his heart. A Democrat to his bone marrow, he was pals with Joe Biden and much of the Democratic establishment. His wife Meryl Gordon (they met at the *Daily*) is a literary biographer who teaches journalism at New York University.

I click on the *Michigan Daily* website from time to time and it is sad what it has become, as feeble as so many of the other formerly great newspapers that it once sought to emulate. It has descended into the pit of publishing trigger warnings on its articles and promoting the cult of transgenderism. It carries no dissenting voices. There's no fun. There's little evident curiosity and much stenographic reporting. The *Daily* has even hived off a supplement for black students, called *Michigan in Color*. The *Daily* is now segregated! The lead story when I glanced at it recently: 'UMich commemorates international day for the elimination of racism with theatre performance.'

In media content analysis, what isn't covered is often more revealing than what is. When the University hired the biggest DEI (diversity equity inclusion) team in American academia, it entirely escaped the attention of the *Daily*. I still have a few friends on the faculty. They tell me stories of turmoil within the university faculty and administration of which the *Daily* is entirely unaware. Like much of the once well-regarded American college press, it is mainly a website now. A very poor website, it should be noted. There's no interaction. Minimal innovation. They've sold off the presses and hired a contract printer to produce a weekly paper. It's embarrassing. Trite writing. A shit show. Woke, woke, woke. Weak, weak, weak.

When I passed by the *Daily* on my last visit to Michigan a couple of years ago, in search of lost time, the building was locked. It never had been before. No longer at the centre of campus life, the once proud *Daily* has literally and metaphorically shut the door and has become the butt of derision. The jokes make themselves. 'The *Daily*'s idea of investigative journalism is asking the dining hall why they ran out of vegan nuggets.' 'A newspaper so obsessed with being woke that it forgot how to be interesting.'

When I visited Detroit and the editor of the *Detroit Free Press* on the same trip, I told him how awful I thought the *Daily* had become. He vehemently disagreed. He told me he thought a great deal of *Daily* graduates. He also told me he had instructed his staff to ignore any criticism of the theory that global warming was the fault of humans. This in a city that's still dependent on the auto industry. So today's graduates have a future, it seems, with Gannett.

I had arrived in America at the dawn of a new era. On July 20, 1969, Neil Armstrong, a naval aviator from Wapakoneta, just across the Ohio border, walked on the Moon. His exploit was relayed to the world on a new Intelsat III satellite. I watched on the television.

It was incomprehensible at the time, magical but remote. I didn't know then that astronauts and satellites would be part of my life, too.

4

NEWSPAPERING

Motor City, Detroit—1972
'I come from Detroit where it's rough and I'm not a smooth talker'—Eminem

I'd learned the basics at the *Michigan Daily*, now it was the big time. Detroit was what in baseball is called The Show, the major league. It was a vivid contrast to leafy Ann Arbor. Detroit was full of poor people, declining neighbourhoods and burned-out buildings. It was ruled by criminals, some of them in City Hall.

At the *Daily* I had already done some freelance work[14] for the *Detroit Free Press*, Michigan's most celebrated newspaper. The *Free Press* had a state-wide circulation and took a considerable interest in the goings-on at Michigan's premier university. And plenty was going on. So their monthly cheques—$65 here, $85 there—had kept me in hamburgers and pitchers of dark beer at the Del-Rio Bar and Grill. When the news editor, Walker Lundy, invited me to spend the summer at the paper as a reporter, I was between my junior and senior (third and fourth) years at the university. This was a dream internship. I felt grown up and thought I was an adult but I wasn't really and spent much of the summer out of my depth. Lundy was from Arkansas and earthy. When I once suggested stupidly to him that it was worth trying anything once, a phrase I'd taken for granted as true, he replied, 'Did you ever fuck a pig?' A memorable correction.

I was awed when I first reported for duty at the magnificent *Free*

Press building with its stone carvings on the facade, of Benjamin Franklin and the journalist Horace Greeley.[15] Even the lobby was overwhelming, featuring a gilded sculpture by Ulysses A. Ricci of the goddesses of Commerce and Communication. I could hardly believe that I was to be paid to work here. This was one of the most fabled newspapers in America. It had just won a Pulitzer Prize, the pinnacle of professional recognition. And it had a voice, a style of its own, which thrilled me.

Although it wasn't obvious at the time, all this would turn to dust. The magnificent building is now a mixed use office building and condominium. I was there just before the inexorable decline of newspapers began. One of the very last to experience this life. The rise of the internet and mobile devices would meltdown the entire industry and the journalism it had sustained.

So I was lucky to be part of this world before it was gone, not that I then knew it would be. I was but a worker ant, and not especially important, but I had a fantastic view of the passing caravanserai.

The *Free Press* saw itself as defiant and principled and was genuinely a brazen, gutsy big-city American newspaper. With roots in abolitionism and the campaign for free public education, the paper was progressive and crusading. The *Free Press* stood for its readers. It was scrappy and fearless.

I was given a press card and under my byline in agate type I was identified as a *Free Press* Staff Writer. It was amazing. Hundreds of thousands of people reading MY story with MY name on it! This was to be a thrill that never grew stale. I would have done this for nothing. That summer I wrote some not bad feature stories, with a lot of help from the talented rewrite men, who turned my chicken shit into publishable chicken salad. But mainly I worked the police beat. I'd seen movies like His Girl Friday and Deadline USA. This was the real thing.

The *Free Press* newsroom was stuffed with talent, and although the paper was a champion of civil rights, the staff would pass no contemporary DEI test. I don't remember a single reporter or editor of colour in this overwhelmingly black city. The managing editor was Neal Shine, a legendary Detroit newspaperman; his executive editor was Kurt Luedtke, who wrote screenplays on the side, and was later to win an Academy Award for Out of Africa. His film Absence of Malice starring Sally Field was a brutal exposé of newspaper ethics. William Schmidt was the star reporter, he later moved on to the London Bureau of the *New York Times*. Brilliant Jo Thomas was there writing about behaviour, which was a fruitful brief in Detroit. She also moved on to the *New York Times*. Did she have some 'thing' with Luedtke? She had a dog named Kurt. Jo Thomas was a hard-as-nails reporter who exposed corruption in the Teamsters Union. Her memoir, *Striving: Adventures of a Female Journalist in a Man's World*, (99 Cups of Coffee Publishing Company, 2023) details her experiences as a pioneering female journalist navigating a predominantly male industry.

Howard Kohn, himself a *Daily* alumnus was a star reporter before he was exposed as a fantasist, inventing his own kidnapping.

They all seemed like Gods to me. Upstairs, in the tower, the *New York Times* maintained a two-man bureau headed by Jerry Flint, the doyen of Detroit auto industry reporters and the most cynical journalist I ever met. His verdict on the famous automotive Dodge family was that they were 'trash.' The job of a mayor when a city was flooding was to be photographed filling sandbags, he noted. His solution to the cruise missile debate of the time was the nuclear-armed 'cruise Volkswagen' which would be lined up on the East German border and in the event of war, sent on cruise control to the east, and 'some would get through.' Flint later became a columnist for *Forbes* business magazine which allowed him wider scope to indulge his sense of humour, in a way that the *New York Times* would not. The magazine was owned by Malcolm Forbes, also a larger-than-life figure, who had a jet named The Capitalist Tool.

Flint was assisted by Agis Salpukas, who was also an extraordinary journalist, but personally tormented. He eventually killed himself. We became friends and he came to Ann Arbor and mentored us at the *Michigan Daily*, and had a fling with one of our editors. I hung out with these guys a lot. We used to eat dinner at the Detroit Press Club, alas long gone. The press club made historic hamburgers.

I was paid $168 per week, the union minimum, which was a fortune at the time, when gasoline was 30 cents a gallon and a bag of groceries cost $10. But Detroit was a mess. During the 1967 uprising against heavy-handed police, 43 people were killed, and the *Free Press* won its Pulitzer Prize. There were more riots in 1968, following the assassination of Martin Luther King. Detroit was destroyed as a viable city.

David Maraniss wrote a very long and dull book[16] documenting Detroit's struggles in such pointillist detail that a great story became a slog. Americans have a tendency to write too long and only a few, like Robert Caro, can master it. The unreadable book was nevertheless widely praised by American reviewers and it is at least a definitive memorial to the formerly great city.

My fly-on-the-wall view is not as punctilious as that of Maraniss, rather an eyewitness, impressionistic recollection of a city having a nervous breakdown. In 1972 it was already apparent that the riots hadn't been some sort of unfortunate interlude, a mere transient crisis. They had changed the city forever. Detroit after the riots didn't look like it was temporarily at the bottom of a cycle. The damage was enduring.

Whites took fright and fled to the suburbs, which boomed. Before the riots, the city was never integrated. There were black neighbourhoods and white neighbourhoods. Now, there were only black neighbourhoods. Poor black neighbourhoods, mostly. Whites and affluent blacks were abandoning the city and by 1972, the flight from Detroit was complete, entire neighbourhoods were abandoned, the city was on its knees, and it was to get worse. Gangsters were fighting over the spoils. It was a city gone to hell but a paradise for journalists.

Detroit's newspaper culture has disappeared though the city is looking a little better now, having crawled back from the brink. Awful Gannett has destroyed everything, as it always does. The *Free*

Press newsroom in Detroit is now housed in an empty, soulless office space in an anonymous downtown building. The *New York Times* has closed its bureau.

When I got there in 1972 The *Detroit Free Press* with its paid circulation of half a million was a formidable actor. These were the last days of newspapers powered by manual typewriters and linotype machines.[17] Journalists still wore hats, compositors made pages out of lead, pots of glue were on the night city desk.

The feisty morning *Free Press* was then still owned by the benevolent old-school publisher Knight Newspapers, a respected family group including the *Philadelphia Inquirer* and *Miami Herald*. Knight's merger with Ridder Newspapers in 1974 was the first step on the road to damnation. Detroit was then a real two-newspaper town. There was also the staid but mighty *Detroit News*, published by the family-owned Evening News Association. The *News* sold close to 600,000 copies daily. It subsequently fell to Gannett.

In August 2005, as part of a larger transaction, Gannett bought the *Detroit Free Press* from Knight Ridder, while the Detroit *News* was sold by Gannett to MediaNews Group, a hedge fund-backed media conglomerate known for aggressive cost cutting.

Back then, oblivious to the imminent consolidations, rationalisations and mismanagement to come, the *Free Press* and the *News* were fierce rivals. I felt like I was an extra in a movie. There were copy editors who wore green eye shades. Some of them were old enough to remember the Purple Gang.[18] Dead copy was smashed onto the spike. Detroit was still the fifth largest news market in America. Newspapers were supremely relevant, stuffed with display ads, coupons and classifieds and with news, sports and business news.

Local television news was still relatively crude. There were no helicopters or satellite trucks or digital cameras. The TV boys copied newspaper stories. While our presses were rolling, the TV lot were off developing their film, if they had any. The newspapers were the supreme source of news.

The only local rival to *Free Press* and *Detroit News* hegemony was

CKLW radio, the self-declared Big 8, a 50,000 watt, clear-channel MW/AM station in Windsor, Ontario, across the heaving Detroit river. Although the station was licensed in Canada, it was the rocking signature sound of the Motor City, playing Motown and percussive pop. Its signal was so powerful that if atmospheric conditions were right, it could reputedly be heard in Finland.

The news team at CKLW were the last of the unabashedly tabloid-mentality radio journalists who would today be compelled by the Human Resources Department to take remedial sensitivity training. The station's blood-curdling commentary was legendary.[19] The writing and delivery were uninhibited and arresting, combining shock, horror and perverse glee. To the background sound of chatting teletype machines, CKLW News bulletins were finely tuned to the slaughter on the streets. Ding! Ding! Ding! The bells rang.

'Accommodations are getting tighter at the Wayne County morgue where officials are staring at sixteen new feet poking up from under those green rubber blankets... after eight murders since midnight... they were shot through the head...'.

So this was the setting for my journalism journey in Detroit. Down in the trenches, on the police beat, getting gory details to the news desk before the *News* or CKLW had them was the basic requirement of the job. I was a leg man, in the parlance. The lowest rung on the ladder.

The grimy press room at police headquarters was conveniently located next to the morgue. The coroner used to invite me over for autopsies. I squeamishly declined. There were two desks. Two chairs. There was a police phone that would connect on a private network with all the outposts of the department. I'd call the precincts, chat with the desk sergeant at each one, trying to conceal my British accent. Because I called on a police phone they were often pretty forthcoming. But the action was usually elsewhere and I was rarely at headquarters, dispatched by the city desk[20] to the scene of the latest outrage. My prized press pass even let me cross police and fire lines, which let me get up close, to scoop up the colour from neighbours and cops.

Although most unfortunate for those killed, the summer of 1972 was the best of times for the news desks. It was non-stop bang bang action (705 murders and rising—835 the year after). 'Wonderful story' was the cry of Nicky the deputy city (news) editor as copy passed before her, reporting a particularly gruesome crime.

A particularity of the gang war in the city that year was the fly-in hitmen. They jetted into town, killed their victims, stole their cars, usually a Lincoln, the marque favoured at that time by the criminal community, dumped the corpses in the capacious trunk, and dropped the vehicle into the long-term parking lot at the Detroit Wayne County Metropolitan airport. Inevitably the corpse would betray itself. It didn't take long, as it was a very hot summer. The executioner was long gone.

Business was good for ice cream trucks, too, which had installed police radio scanners so they could get to the urban crime scenes fast, to serve up refreshments to the crowds that had gathered as the coroner's men removed the bodies. The ice cream was good. America is truly a land of enterprise.

Journalism is all about telling stories but the big picture depends on the details. It was at the *Free Press* that I learned the power of specificity from Jim Dewey, a very kind night city editor who read Pascal when he was not employed rewriting dispatches from reporters in the field. He taught me to notice that fresh blood did not merely spill on the floor of a recently robbed Savings and Loan, but onto the *green tile floor*. Dewey taught me another lesson. 'Never trust the cops. Or anyone. Investigate everything yourself, as if it all depends on you.'

After work, journalists, cops, pols and gamblers would gather at the Anchor Bar and Grill, around the corner from the newspaper offices. Here, plots were made, reporters gloated over their victories and drowned the misery of defeat. Sporting investments were meanwhile laid from the wall of pay phones—this was before mobiles.[21]

The Anchor was the home bar of the legendary Detroit police chief Ray Girardin. Legendary because he ascended into this role from his previous job as the chief police reporter for the Detroit News. This is how crazy and cinematic it was in Detroit. A city where a journalist could be promoted from police reporter to police chief.

The *Free Press* had whetted my appetite for journalism and there was no doubt it would be my life, although everything was soon to change and my career didn't turn out as I might have expected. But I wasn't yet done with newspapers.

5

THE STICKS

Ohio—1973

'A, O, oh, way to go, Ohio'—The Pretenders.

Jobs for journalists were easy to get in 1973 and the graduating *Michigan Daily* staff dispersed to join papers all over America, many going on to great things and glittering prizes. But the *Free Press* wasn't hiring. Or so they said. I think I had maybe pissed off one of the deputy city editors but maybe they just weren't hiring. It was a good thing to be cast into the wilderness and eventually I landed well. I was always lucky, although sometimes it is said that you make your own luck so possibly it was my troublemaking that got me noticed. I'd done some freelance stories as the University of Michigan campus correspondent for the *New York Times*, a gig I'd landed via Jerry Flint, the *New York Times* bureau chief in Detroit. I got a lot into the paper. I got a huge show for one about an off-campus dorm where male and female students shared bedrooms in a social experiment of sexual equality, they claimed. It made the 'second front page' where the paper displayed its feature of the day. Even the Gray Lady had a taste for the salacious. The president of the university told me the article had cost $1 million in cancelled alumni contributions. I seem to remember I was paid $100 for the story.

On the strength of this, David Jones, the national editor, offered me a job as a news assistant in New York, which was then the entry level. Or I could get seasoned in the provinces and come back later, he said, recommending the latter. That sounded like a better idea. Much as the *New York Times* was the greatest newspaper in America, I wanted to get reporting, not spend a year or two fetching other people's copy. And bingo. The *Cincinnati Post*, a Scripps-Howard afternoon paper in Ohio, was recruiting. They flew me down for an interview. The *Cincinnati Post* no longer exists, which is no great loss as it was a terrible newspaper. Its building has since been demolished and an apartment block stands in its place.

Cincinnati seemed a pleasant city, prosperous, bourgeois. It boasted the headquarters of Proctor and Gamble. It was a historic Ohio River trading post. Appalachia was on the doorstep. Covington, Kentucky was just the other side of the Ohio River. Colonel Sanders invented Kentucky Fried Chicken there.

I took the job they offered because they were charming at the time and joined the paper as a general assignment reporter. I never clicked. From the first day it felt like a mistake. The paper was exhausted. The *Post* was located in a then-grimy neighbourhood east of downtown. It looks better now, on Google Street View. The tavern opposite was the hangout. The printers drank a shot and a beer for breakfast. Cincinnati was a serious city but Scripps-Howard was a miserable operator. On no account was offense to be given to any friend of the proprietor, who lived in a squalid mansion in the Cincinnati hills. I was at his house once. He was a hoarder. Every square inch was heaped in yellowing newspapers.

The editors were local men, not keen to make a stir. The corporate culture was stinginess. You had to get permission to make a long-distance call. To get a new pencil you had to hand in the stub of an old one. No wonder they were recruiting. Nobody wanted to work there. The editors were miserable men, to put it generously. They liked breezy features boosting civic pride but shied away from rocking the boat, which is what I'd wanted to do.

Cincinnati prided itself on respectability but as is often the case, public trust conceals private lust. The *Post* was scooped when the city councillor Jerry Springer—yes, him—was caught writing a check to pay a prostitute. It was the morning paper, the *Cincinnati Enquirer*,[22] that broke the story. The scandal didn't obstruct Springer's subsequent rise to even greater fame, first re-elected to the council as mayor, later as a notorious chat show host. Beneath the respectable veneer of old Cincinnati there were lots of scams waiting to be exposed.

That wasn't going to happen at the *Cincinnati Post*. The city of Cincinnati and its hinterlands were fertile territory but the *Post* had no discernible soul, guts or interest in a fight. When what I wanted to do was provoke. I came across a story of corruption in the police department. A bent detective was taking bribes from a notorious drug dealer, I learned. The story looked hard to do but solid and deliverable. The editors shut it down. I wasn't there long. After a few months, now married to my university sweetheart, we moved 50 miles north, to the city of Dayton and, for me, a job as a reporter on the *Dayton Daily News*. The *Daily News* was a serious newspaper, in another league. The newsroom atmosphere was buzzy not morose. The editors were not brain dead. You could take as many pencils as you wanted. A real newspaper was being produced.

The *Daily News* was an illustrious title founded in 1898 by James M. Cox, twice Democratic governor of Ohio. It was still owned by the Cox family, who grew the Dayton paper into what's now Cox Enterprises, the umbrella for one of the great American media and cable TV dynasties. Dayton was a newsy city, despite the observation by the writer Chitra Banerjee Divakaruni, the Indian poet, who attended university there: 'I came to the plain fields of Ohio with pictures painted by Hollywood movies and the works of Tennessee Williams and Arthur Miller. None of them had much to say, if at all, about Dayton.' That's not really fair.

Dayton in its day was at the centre of the engineering revolution that propelled American industrial power, though this was now on the cusp of decline. The Wright Brothers built their first airplane in their bicycle shop here. The automobile revolution moved to a higher gear when the starter motor was invented in Dayton. National Cash Register supplied the world from its factories before closing them and moving to Atlanta to focus on ATM machines and software.

Dayton has a special place in newspaper lore. Ben Hecht, the Chicago reporter turned screenwriter and author of the classic newspaper Broadway play then movie *His Girl Friday*, came to Dayton to cover the devastating 1913 flood when the Miami River burst its banks killing 400 people. He wrote about it in his book *A Child of the Century*, published in 1954 after a career as a reporter and in Hollywood.

'A dozen telegraph operators were sending out messages. The head operator refused to let me file a story. He had instructions that no message of more than two words was to be sent by any one sender. The messages going out all read the same. 'Am safe.' And a signature was attached. I talked to the head operator, drank hot coffee, heard a hundred fascinating details of the flood—horses swimming into second-floor windows, houses floating away with families on the roofs. 'Can I use your typewriter?' I asked. 'It's no use,' the head operator said. 'You can only file two words.'

Hecht wrote six pages of double-spaced copy on the typewriter, as the telegraph keys kept clicking their 'Am safe' obbligato.

'"Just read it, even if you can't send it," I said to the head operator. He read my copy and tears filled his eyes. His face flushed. When he had finished the last page he called out, "Take a rest, Jim. I'm going to use your key." I had written a story about the heroes of the Miami Junction telegraph station—the twelve men who had sat for thirty hours without leaving their posts, without knowing if their own families were alive or drowned, and tapped out the thousands of happiness-bringing 'Am safe' messages to other relatives. The names and descriptions of each of the twelve heroes were in my story.'

The telegraph office was also central to Evelyn Waugh's novel *Scoop,* when the hapless foreign correspondent William Boot, after arriving in Ishmaelia, sends a hopeless, newsless telegram to the *Daily Beast.* It read:

'NO NEWS AT PRESENT THANKS WARNING ABOUT

CABLING PRICES BUT IVE PLENTY MONEY LEFT AND ANYWAY WHEN I OFFERED TO PAY WIRELESS MAN SAID IT WAS ALL RIGHT PAID OTHER END RAINING HARD HOPE ALL WELL ENGLAND WILL CABLE AGAIN IF ANY NEWS.'

This ineptitude is strongly reflected in the efforts of the inept amateurs cosplaying journalists in today's media. Although the twist in Waugh's tale is that it's Boot who gets the scoop.

When we got to Dayton the Cox family had long left Ohio for Atlanta, where they owned the *Atlanta Journal* and *Atlanta Constitution*[23] and we never saw them, although they kept their Gulfstream jet at the Dayton Municipal Airport.

A contemporary note: James 'Fergie' Chambers, an heir to the family media empire, and self-proclaimed communist, has publicly distanced himself from the family business, criticizing its ties to what he describes as 'rotten capitalism.' His financial contributions to left-wing causes are significant, as he reportedly inherited hundreds of millions of dollars from the Cox family fortune. It's an odd family.

This was all in the future. In 1975, Cox was a benevolent, family proprietor. Their editors were allowed to run a spirited operation that didn't hesitate to annoy the local elite. There was a morning paper, the *Journal-Herald*, and the afternoon *Dayton Daily News*. The papers were commonly owned but editorially competitive. My *Journal-Herald* rival at the courthouse was cute, flirtatious and ruthless. Dayton Newspapers Inc, the holding company, was highly profitable, amidst supermarket price wars driving pages of display advertising and coupons. Then there were pages of classified ads, and a quarter million subscribers paying 20 cents a day to buy it. It was a fine business to be in.

I had a wonderful job and worked amongst many memorable characters. The newsroom was a menagerie of eccentrics. The defence and aviation correspondent Jack Jones never threw anything away. His desk was stacked high with documents. He seemed able to instantly retrieve what he needed from the miden. His focus of coverage was Wright Patterson Air Force Base outside of town. It was a centre for many newsworthy activities and Jones broke lots of national stories. It was also reported that the base was being used to store alien wreckage from a UFO crash—a story that Jones pooh-poohed.

The entertainment and 'after dark' correspondent, Bernie Wulkotte had mysterious enemies and carried a .38 calibre revolver. His movements were unpredictable. Pete Fusco was a talented feature writer who really wanted to be a professional pilot. He eventually achieved his goal. He later wrote an magnificent memoir of his life in the sky, *Moondog's Academy of the Air* (iUniverse, 2000), in which he charted his ascent from a feature writer on the *Dayton Daily News* to a jobbing cargo pilot, hauling mysterious cargo, then a DC-10 captain for Continental Airlines.

There was George Smith, a great story-getter who was on staff for but three months before mysteriously vanishing, pursued by cops, who showed up in the newsroom with an arrest warrant. He broke a wonderful story about ticket fixing before disappearing without even a puff of smoke.

Jimmy Carter came to see us when he was scoping his bid for the presidency and I spent two hours with him in the boardroom, that was once the Governor's office. I liked him. He seemed not mad. But I was naive. He'd been an engineering officer in the navy, working for the legendary Jewish Admiral Hyman Rickover, father of America's nuclear navy. Someone I later profiled in the *New Republic*. But while I have a lot of respect for engineers, they can have limitations. Sometimes they get bogged down in the weeds. Prosecutors don't like them on juries. Carter, who was a good man, wasn't a great president. He was scheduling the White House tennis court as the ayatollah returned to Tehran.

In Dayton, we were 'hicks in the sticks', far from any of the major media centres, in the flyover country of archetypal middle America, but our paper had talent, integrity and flair.

My principal beat was the Montgomery County Common Pleas Court, which was a young journalist's mother lode. Revolting crimes, sordid scandals, tall tales. All were abundant. The courtrooms were theatrical. 'Were you shot in the fracas?', a lawyer asked a witness one day. 'No, Sir, just below the belly button.'

Unlike in Britain where you have to fight for every scrap of information, I got to read every piece of paper filed with the clerk's office, which was a paper tray that was a bottomless source of stories. These were the days when people still trusted reporters and talked to us. I hung out with the prosecutors and cops, and wandered in and out of the judges' chambers. After the closing gavel, judges, prosecutors, defence lawyers and court reporters would assemble in chief judge Kessler's chambers for a whiskey. He kept a spittoon by his desk, a cigar in his jaws and hens at his farm. They produced green eggs, which he would gift to his cronies. These sessions were where he literally held court, telling wacky stories. He was a bit of a Sam Ervin[24] character, revelling in his persona as a simple country lawyer. Asked about a recent case, he told of a hillbilly farmer who whacked his mule with a plank. 'Why?' he was asked. 'To get his attention.' This was also Judge Kessler's sentencing philosophy.

I landed some monumental scoops in Dayton. When two federal agents had a shootout in the federal building, one killing the other, I used the new Freedom of Information Act to get my hands on the investigative documents. That was the basis for a double-page spread with a splashy front page write-off. When a drug-mule teenage prostitute was arrested, I got her mother to give me her revealing diaries, implicating the police in dealing sex and drugs. Her pimp had a diamond in his tooth. There were lots of names in her little black book including one of the city's most prominent lawyers. Another splash. Although after that one I was no longer persona grata in the Dayton Police detectives' squad room.

Dayton is not the most glamorous part of America, but was a perfect place to be a reporter. The *Daily News* punched above its weight and had a solid national reputation. The city was fading and had plenty of problems, which would get worse, but this only made it more interesting.

When I left Dayton to head for Washington, the first computer terminals had started to appear in the newsroom.

The *Dayton Daily News* no longer exists as a freestanding title. It merged with the *Journal-Herald*, but fortunately evaded Gannett and is still owned by the Cox family. It publishes a physical newspaper six days a week. I can't fully see it from here in France because it hasn't bothered to conform to EU rules hence its content isn't available in Europe.

6

VILE SNAKES

Washington DC—1979
Broadcasting's great wasteland

Mrs Miller graduated from law school in Ohio (first in her class) and we moved to America's capital, or close by. She got sworn in by Justice Potter Stewart, an Ohioan, at the United States Supreme Court. We rented a tiny townhouse in Alexandria, Virginia, which was a little way out, then after a few months moved closer in, to an apartment in Arlington, where we could look over the Potomac River to see the Washington Monument and Lincoln Memorial. She took a job as an attorney in the enforcement division of the Securities and Exchange Commission. Oil and gas investment fraud was rampant and dentists with spare cash were being fleeced. She would go on to prosecute the celebrated Korean Unification Church leader Reverend Sun Myung Moon for securities fraud. I declared myself a freelancer. Which was a cover for being unemployed.

Washington was heady, and trading the Montgomery County, Ohio Courthouse for the Capitol and White House was thrilling. This made even Detroit seem provincial. But I had no job. I was by now an experienced newspaper reporter but I was a D.C. baby. I'd have to see what turned up. At least I had contacts.

Washington had attracted many of my *Michigan Daily* cohort. Some were working for Jimmy Carter, the new president. After the traumas of the Vietnam War and Watergate, there was a lot of optimism about Carter. Patricia Bauer, another in the mafia of *Michigan Daily* colleagues, was working as the editor of the White House news summary, a daily digest of the nation's newspapers distributed to the President and his staff. She invited me to lunch in the White House Mess, where the food was good. We were surrounded by the great political personalities of the new administration.

Disappointment has been constant when I have foolishly had faith in politicians. Carter at least was well meaning and not corrupt but the job overwhelmed him. He couldn't see the big picture for the details. He stumbled from one crisis to another, terminating in the hostage taking in Iran and the botched attempted rescue raid on Tehran in April 1980.[25]

Now as it so happened, and this is central to developments henceforth, the 1980s were also the time when communications technology exploded. The first domestic television relay satellites were being launched. Cable television boomed. There were suddenly computer stores on M Street. I took an early laptop, a Radio Shack TRS-80,[26] to an ITU conference in Switzerland and filed copy over a modem that used a rubber cup to cover the telephone mouthpiece. I wasn't the first or only journalist to figure out that technology was going to unsettle the media business. But as has often been the case in my career, I was in the right place at the right time and observed the revolution up close. I was technically more curious than most journalists, who then as now are more obsessed with political gossip than the electromagnetic frequency spectrum. I talked to engineers who had a clear-sighted view of what was coming as well as the politicians, industry actors and regulators. 'Talk to the engineers,' is another of my Rules for Journalism. This was what led to my fateful crossing of paths with Rupert Murdoch.

The freelance market was good but I needed a permanent gig because as an unknown writer. I was spending as much time pitching ideas as writing and cheques were scarce. I wrote stories for the *New Republic,* profiling Robert MacNamara amongst others, but was hearing some incredible stories from yet another *Michigan Daily* colleague, who was working in one of the network bureaus in

Washington. The amount of money sloshing around the three television networks was so huge that they had to hide it, in gigantic salaries and corporate jets. Something smelled. The airwaves were supposed to belong to the public but they had become a magic money tree for the privileged market participants. From being a courthouse reporter in Ohio, I was becoming a media journalist in Washington, growing ever more curious about the TV business and the media business generally.

My view was that broadcasting in America was a complete stitch-up, enriching the politically connected who had broadcast licenses, who were mainly serving a cornucopia of trash to the viewers. The industry employed thuggish lobbyists in Washington to keep the Congress on side. This was the hustle of Lady Bird Johnson, whose initial investment of $17,500 in a Texas radio station grew into a fortune, estimated at over $150 million.

I conceitedly considered it my mission to bring down the vile snakes who owned television stations. An animus I subsequently transferred to the BBC. Editors were less timorous in those days. I contributed to *Channels of Communication*, founded by the John and Mary Markle Foundation, edited by Les Brown, the former TV editor of the *New York Times*. He took one look at my copy and announced, 'I'm going to teach you how to write'. He was right to spot my weakness. It was a giant leap from the clipped newspaper style I had mastered to the much more sophisticated style of magazines. I was clearing my throat as a writer. I had still to find a writerly voice. He was a good teacher, and encouraged my troublemaking instincts. Brown had a healthy contempt for the broadcasters, bred from familiarity. I went on to expose the Washington influence machine of the television network lobbyists in *TV Guide*, at that time the largest selling magazine in America. They paid $3,000 for a feature, a small fortune then.

What I discovered was that the hunger of politicians for airtime had made the broadcasters untouchable. The politicians protected the broadcasters from competition and the broadcasters returned the favour. It was a symbiotic and toxic relationship. The losers were the public who theoretically owned the electromagnetic broadcasting spectrum that had become a 'vast wasteland,' in the words of Newt Minow, a former chairman of the Federal Communications Commission. He had told American broadcasters in 1961:

'…when television is bad, nothing is worse. I invite each of you to sit down in front of your television set when your station goes on the air and stay there for a day, without a book, without a magazine, without a newspaper, without a profit-and-loss sheet, or a rating book to distract you. Keep your eyes glued to that set until the station signs off. I can assure you that what you will observe is a vast wasteland. You will see a procession of game shows, formula comedies about totally unbelievable families, blood and thunder, mayhem, violence, sadism, murder, Western badmen, Western good men, private eyes, gangsters, more violence…'

There were some honourable exceptions but Minow's criticism was still valid. I started my attack on the broadcasters advocating radical regulatory surgery on the television system. But it was soon obvious these changes would never happen because of the political power of the industry. The irresistible vector of change would be technological, and most immediately the emerging satellite and cable television channels like HBO that could compete with the established actors, offering new choices.

My conviction that the smug complacent broadcasters were doomed, or at the very least ought to be, brought me into the orbit of Al Warren, an old-school trade journalist, a WWII veteran fascinated by technology since spending the war hunched over radio sets in the Aleutian Islands. After demobilisation from the Navy, he had created a successful boutique publishing company retailing insider news and gossip on what was then the nascent TV industry.

Warren's newsletter thrived through the fifties and sixties with the rise of the broadcast industry but Al Warren could see changes coming and pivoted his publications strongly towards the nascent cable industry. He was a crusty editor of the old school who was always looking forward. 'Why can't I watch television on airplanes', he would demand. Of course, now we can.

Paul Warren, Al's son, had been a newspaper reporter, like me, but at the *Rochester Times-Union* (New York), then a respectable newspaper, now no more. It can be remembered mostly as the first newspaper in what grew into the pernicious Gannett empire.

After proving his mettle elsewhere, Paul had joined his father's business, and his ambition was to move it on. We met for lunch at the Bread Oven restaurant on 19th Street, around the corner from the Federal Communications Commission and the company's townhouse on Jefferson Place. It was kismet—fate, destiny. We saw eye to eye on everything. Laughed at each other's jokes. And had the same idea of applying bare-knuckle newspaper tactics to trade journalism. I was hired and together we conceived and launched a new publication, *Communications Daily*, covering the convergence of media, satellites and telecommunications. It was an immediate hit and we sold thousands of subscriptions at $673 each. Al was generous with raises.

We hired some fantastic reporters. There was plenty of talent around. Paul Travis, a newspaper reporter in Florida who had worked with me on the *Michigan Daily*, joined us to cover every day of the huge AT&T antitrust trial, which resulted in the breakup of the monopoly, further stimulating the telecommunications revolution in America. Our circulation soared again.

Immodest to say but we were indispensable at a time of turmoil in communications. When the Soviet science delegation subscribed, a couple of FBI agents showed up at our office to find out what we were up to. The money was pouring in. Paul and I bought matching company sports cars. We were only 'trade' reporters but the *Wall Street Journal* and *Washington Post* were on the phone to us constantly, hunting for our scoops they could call their own. Our access to politicians and officials was unlimited. Those were days when you could simply walk into the office of a Senator or an agency chairman and just chat. Everyone read us. We were covering space transportation, fibre optics, satellite services and then something called Darpanet—which became the internet—while most reporters were struggling to distinguish an earth station from an earth worm.

Washington was everything I'd expected. I was regularly flying to Tokyo, London, Paris and Geneva, covering stories. There were invitations to the grandest balls. Openings at the Kennedy Center. Unlimited expenses for lunches at the greatest power dining restaurants. Our social life was top tier. We had a backyard barbecue with Al Gore.

Our newsroom had real talent. Often, they were reporters who lacked the Ivy League credentials sought by the *Washington Post* but were hungrier and better for it. We were the trade press, a term often used as a pejorative but often you find trade reporters really doing some digging, instead of regurgitating handouts and posing at press conferences. A bullseye hire was Theresa Foley, a smart reporter who saw through the flannel. She was a blonde girl geek who hung out with admirals and the like. Her beat was aerospace, NASA and the Pentagon. It's certainly not politically correct to say it, but clever, cute, female reporters get stories where male counterparts don't get a look in, especially with males of a certain age, who are in the know. She was a scoop machine and didn't make mistakes.

After the Space Shuttle Challenger disaster in 1986 that killed seven astronauts and mission specialists, she organised a dinner with General Chuck Yeager, the Air Force ace who had broken the sound barrier in 1947, and Colonel Joe Engle, himself an astronaut and shuttle pilot. They were amusing, unpretentious guys. Yeager—the founding member of the group of pilots that Tom Wolfe called the Brotherhood of the Right Stuff—had the classic look of a 20th-century American military hero, square-jawed, fit, sharp, and commanding. He was also just relaxed and funny and though he was a legend wore his celebrity invisibly. Engle had the right-stuff look. Blue-eyed, high cheekbones, lean. We were in an off-the-beaten-track Spanish restaurant on Columbia Road in a neighbourhood little frequented by the famous and nobody recognised them. Theresa and I just listened in awe as the two pilots talked about their days at Edwards Air Force Base, the aircraft they had flown, and the famous broasted chicken at Annie's Restaurant, on the highway running past Edwards, where the test pilots hung out.

But then we got serious and talked about the Challenger. Colonel Engle was the commander on the Space Shuttle Columbia for STS-2 in November 1981, which was the second Space Shuttle mission. What had gone wrong with Challenger?

We knew some of what had happened but not why. There were freezing temperatures at the launch site. An O-ring seal on the right side booster was made brittle by the cold. The seal failed leading to the breach of the enormous external fuel tank and the explosion of liquid hydrogen and oxygen that destroyed the Shuttle itself.

How had this been possible?

General Yeager had a theory. When he broke the sound barrier in the Bell X-1, he explained, it was possible for him and the engineers to understand every component of the vehicle, and how those components fit together and interacted. By the time of the Space Shuttle, 33 years later, it had become humanly impossible for anyone to understand the entirety of the complex vehicle, least of all the pilots, who had to take for granted the advice that it was safe to fly, when clearly it wasn't.

In a nutshell, Yeager argued, humans were building systems so complex they were impossible for humans to understand them in their entirety. That's a chilling and prescient warning for today, in the era of artificial intelligence and incorporating, in theory, the sum of all human knowledge. These systems go far beyond the Billion Dollar Brain imagined by Len Deighton in his novel of 1966,[27] it's a Trillion Dollar Brain. The question must be quite seriously posed: What could possibly go wrong?

At our headquarters on Jefferson Place, just around the corner from the FCC, missing the buzz of newspapers, Paul and I had built a real newsroom for ourselves. We dumped the typewriters and installed Wang word processors. We put a satellite dish on the roof of the building. It wasn't connected to anything. We were showing off. We had a good table at the White House Correspondents Dinner. We knew everything, talked to everyone and we lived well. And this was when Rupert Murdoch came into my life.

Tipped by a 'source' at the Federal Communications

Commission (time to fess up: the source of the story was the FCC's chairman), I broke the story that Murdoch was becoming an American citizen, his naturalisation being rushed through so he could legally buy the for-sale Fox broadcast television stations. To hold a broadcast licence in America, citizenship was obligatory. This was his first move to be a player in the American television industry and a modest if routine scoop but it was picked up by everyone and got Rupert's attention. He promptly subscribed to our newsletter.

These were heady days as awareness grew, among those taking the trouble to pay attention, that everything we had thought about satellites was wrong. The space age was throwing off a gigantic civil application. Reliable Delta rockets were orbiting a new generation of satellites that would completely overturn the television industry

Arthur C. Clarke's 1945 idea of launching communications relays to earth-synchronous orbit was achieved by Nasa in 1963 and the idea was commercialised with the subsequent creation of Intelsat as a global consortium of mostly state-owned telecommunications companies. Arthur and I corresponded. He was very excited about direct-to-home satellite broadcasting, and also the idea for a space elevator[28] for low-cost space transportation. So I looked into it.

By then, communications satellites were taken for granted but the mindset was that they could only usefully used for trunking connections, using massive ground stations like Goonhilly Down with 30 metre antennas.

The first to notice the improving satellites was the American cable television industry, which rapidly installed tens of thousands of 3m dishes, enabling local cable systems to offer dozens of new channels. This is when HBO entered the market, transmitting by satellite a network previously restricted to a complex, restrictive and territorially limited microwave relay.

But as the signs on French level crossing warn, one train can conceal another. Satellite communications was about to take another great leap forward, with more powerful satellites and more sophisticated ground receivers enabling dishes to shrink to 60 centimetres, a size that fits readily on the side of a house.

Incredibly, broadcasters like the BBC in Britain and the Big Three American networks ABC, CBS and NBC, did not understand what this technology would do to them. In America and Europe satellites were about to open the technical capability for direct-to-home satellite television services. They would completely bypass traditional TV transmission networks with their enormous investments in terrestrial equipment, and their inherent limitations on channel capacity due to their use of the scarce UHF television band. Satellites were going to smash the monopoly of the terrestrial television broadcasters, and they didn't see it coming. But I did.

I went to New Jersey, to the RCA Astro high bays where the latest satellites were being built. I talked as usual to the engineers because they are the ones who think around the next corner. This is true in rockets, software, everything. The president of Astro held nothing back. He explained the advances in low-noise devices that made it possible for tiny ground stations to receive and amplify signals from satellites in the geosynchronous orbit, 22,300 miles above the equator. And the new satellites they were building were going to change the world. It was going to be possible to beam dozens, then hundreds of channels direct to homes.

The story I got in New Jersey was that technology was going to kick apart all existing regulatory assumptions and blow open the television industry. It was a Eureka moment although I did not run naked through the streets of Syracuse, like Archimedes. It did, however, define much of what happened next.

7

INSURRECTIONS

Wapping and Isleworth—1986
'Freedom of the press is guaranteed only to those who own one'—A. J.
Liebling.

In 1986, I returned to London, the city where I'd grown up, after an absence of 17 years. Murdoch had smashed the print unions and *The Times* was hiring. It was a Dick Whittington moment. London was buzzing. A wall of money had descended on the City. Margaret Thatcher was turning a fire hose on the cobwebs.

I had left *Communications Daily* in Washington though I probably could have stayed there forever and bought a big house in McLean. I was still having fun. Paul and I and our wives had become friends, and still are, but he was the son of the boss and I was not. I saw other fish to fry. I wanted to move beyond trade journalism, leavened as it was by freelancing for the *Washington Post* and *International Herald Tribune*. Perhaps I was a little homesick. I'd left London reluctantly. This was a homecoming.[29] And the time was right. After years of inexorable decline, making me glad to be in America, there was an undeniable British moment, a renewed dynamism, the possibility of an opening economy.

Mrs Miller was ready for a new adventure, too. With her experience of securities regulation, she integrated quickly into the legal scene in the new City, which was in the throes of the financial Big Bang. She was involved in this until she joined the legal team for the

London 2012 Olympic Games.

The big bang in the media market was perfect for me. Just as Thatcher was clearing up the mess in Britain, Murdoch was cleaning up the mess on Fleet Street. But Britain was trailing America in new channels and revolution was in the air.

On January 24, 1986, Murdoch began printing *The Times*, the *Sunday Times*, the *Sun* and the *News of the World* at his new fortified production site in Wapping. I cheered. I'd visited a friend at the *Financial Times* a year earlier and was horrified what they were putting up with.

Before Rupert smashed them, the print unions in and around Fleet Street (where most major UK newspapers were based) had such control over the production process that if a journalist inadvertently touched a page form (the Stone, in the nomenclature) in the composing room, the chapel would call a meeting and disrupt production. Newspapers could lose an entire night's production on the whim of a shop steward. Whether the paper got out depended how bolshy they were feeling, on the night.

Murdoch put an end to it by using the new legislation Thatcher had introduced. The 1980s had seen a technological upheaval in newspaper production, with the introduction of offset printing and computer typesetting with journalists inputting their copy directly into terminals, eliminating the need for re-typing by union compositors. The composition craft was highly skilled but its end was inevitable. As the unions had been behaving badly for some time, it was more painful than it needed to have been. But the printers were intransigent. Murdoch's patience snapped. British newspapers were dying, and years behind their American homologues in the use of the technologies that could save them.

Murdoch chose the site in Wapping in the Docklands area east of the City and as discreetly as possible, filled it with modern presses and an imported Atex computer system. It was in plain sight, but the unions hadn't anticipated the audacity of their foe.

As the first papers rolled off the presses in Wapping, there was rioting in the streets outside. Mrs Thatcher made sure there were plenty of police. The unions, the National Graphical Association, the Society of Graphical and Allied Trades and the Amalgamated Union of Engineering Workers organised pickets. The dispute became violent, with 1200 arrests. The strike ended in February 1987, with the unions conceding defeat—a colossal blow to union power in the UK and a gigantic boost to the ambition of Murdoch.

As the pickets raged, I flew to London for an interview with Charlie Wilson, the editor of *The Times*. It was a fabled newspaper. I wasn't confident. I had most recently been a mere trade-press reporter in Washington. But I was lucky. He was in a hiring frenzy because many of his journalists had walked out rather than cross the picket lines. He needed specialists. Somewhat to my surprise, I was hired on the spot as media correspondent.

But the editor and I didn't see eye to eye. When I told him technology was going to drive huge changes in media he laughed, pointed at his Atex terminal and replied that the technology story had already happened, it was over.

Oh dear. Charlie was an alumnus of the *Daily Mail* and still thought television was mostly about celebrities. Charlie therefore wanted me to cover showbusiness. I wouldn't know a celebrity if one sat next to me. I suspect he only hired me because Rupert had signalled royal assent.

Rupert had already parlayed his Australian inheritance into the big footprint of News Corporation in London, New York and now Los Angeles with his move on 20th Century Fox. Quick-witted, single-minded, he usually got his way. Now, victorious at Wapping, the sky was the limit.

In America, the multi-channel television revolution was already underway, mainly through cable connections. Britain however was virgin territory. There were 20 daily and Sunday national newspapers but only four TV channels. While the established broadcasters slept, Rupert schemed.

The key to his plan was the planned launch of the Luxembourg Astra satellite, made by my engineer friends at RCA Astro in New Jersey, although the name on the door had changed to GE

Aerospace. It was a capable modern satellite that could transmit 24 simultaneous television channels to a 60cm dish. Leasing four of these channels from Astra, Murdoch would kick down the door of the British television market that had not welcomed him as a member. But it remained to be launched.

Clueless on show business, I wasn't getting on with Charlie Wilson at *The Times* and was fortuitously rescued by Andrew Neil. Andrew brought me on to the *Sunday Times* as media editor. It was a fancier title, came with more money and I would have two pages to fill each week. Andrew was a geek before geeks were cool. He was fascinated by technology. Private Eye said at the time that if he couldn't plug it in, he wasn't interested.

I'd known Andrew for years, from when I was working on a project for the *Economist* in Washington, and he was an editor in London. He said he'd liked my bare-knuckle approach to American broadcasters and thought it might stir things up to turn me loose on the British ones. This became a productive partnership. Later, when Murdoch parachuted Andrew into Sky as chief executive, he took me with him.

Sky, with or without a satellite, was a potential disaster in the making. It was a damn close-run thing. As media editor of the *Sunday Times*, I had been watching its clumsy birthing with horror. The new campus at Isleworth in West London was a building site. They were building or trying to build studios and offices and a canteen and an uplink centre, installing sensitive electronic equipment in clouds of dust.

The project was coming under political attack from those who had finally twigged that Murdoch's project was completely unregulated, a lawless operation in a regime that had simply not anticipated that what Sky intended to do was even possible.

But Sky's management was making unforced errors. And looking stupid. They'd even launched an advertising campaign boasting that 'Sky is revolting'. They thought this clever. Sky with its promise to double the number of channels overnight looked like a cowboy start-up, without a chance in hell.

I was a gung-ho partisan for competitive television, making no apologies for loathing the BBC-ITV-Channel 4 triopoly. Amongst my peers in the media press I was isolated in this opinion. I was even attacked by *Private Eye*, the regime's satirist. The Hack Watch column bestowed on me the moniker 'Not Dr Jonathan' to avoid confusion with Dr Jonathan Miller, the polymath and BBC stalwart, who complained to the *Sunday Times* that I had usurped his good reputation. Possibly I had. One reader sent me a libretto he had written and wanted to know if I was interested in producing it at the Royal Opera House.

With Andrew at my back, I wasn't bothered. I was a willing conscript in Andrew's project to blow apart the British TV market. While every other media correspondent was devoted to exactly the opposite cause, grovelling to the BBC.

Being media editor of the *Sunday Times* was a blast because I relished disruption and so did Andrew. Unlike Washington, where everyone talked, in London information was traded strictly transactionally—*do ut des*. I was rude about the BBC In retaliation the BBC press office delighted in handing stories to my competitors, especially Raymond Snoddy of the *Financial Times*, who would later be given an MBE and his own BBC show. The media journalists of the time were described by Andrew Neil as the whores of Fleet Street. Perhaps a little harsh. Their horizons were limited. They traded access for obedience and so kept the showbiz stories flowing and their editors happy. The privileged got invited onto BBC chat shows and received cheques.

At the *Sunday Times*, Andrew and I produced a series of scoops that deeply embarrassed the broadcasters. I pursued BBC director general John Birt to New Mexico and got an exclusive interview in which he confessed that the corporation was grossly over-staffed. It was a front-page splash. I tracked down another DG, Michael Checkland, to Botswana, where he was on safari at licence-fee payers expense. It was officially a meeting of the Commonwealth Broadcasting Association, made up of BBC-like broadcasters. He refused to talk to me.

And not just the BBC. When the cross-channel ferry the Herald of Free Enterprise sank in Zeebrugge harbour in 1987 we discovered that a cameraman for TV-am, the ITV breakfast franchise, had claimed £92,000 in overtime for a few days work. TV-am's press office denied it but since our source was Bruce Gyngell, the station's managing director, we held firm.

There were but four TV networks on the air in Britain in 1988. The officially-sanctioned British Satellite Broadcasting was to introduce a five-channel satellite that would, by design, keep pesky newcomers off the platform. It was licensed and sponsored by the Independent Broadcasting Authority, a hapless regulator that later became Ofcom, which has proved equally awful. Murdoch was intending to double the number overnight, and open the door to anyone else willing to enter the market. Murdoch had chosen to use a satellite with room for two dozen channels initially, twice that later, and ultimately hundreds more with digital transmission.

Technical standards regulation is often used to distort competition, freezing innovation.[30] The EU had its own agenda for satellite broadcasting, demanding a patented hybrid analogue-digital transmission system called D2MAC dreamed up by the French and Dutch companies Thomson and Philips. They stood to make a fortune from it. And the broadcast establishment liked it too, because it would hugely reduce the number of channels that could be transmitted over a satellite, limiting competition. But I helped head this off, too. Again, the engineers were the key source. The analogue transmission of television was doomed. An EU regulation requiring an analogue system would put Europe years behind the rest of the world.[30] I flew to Washington and penetrated the lab where a 100% digital system was being perfected, permitting hundreds of new channels. I circulated a report to dozens of EU officials and commissioners, joined an alliance with other commercial broadcasters in Europe and together we killed D2MAC.

Sky's ready-to-go satellite technology was superior to the competition. I was not so sure that the Australian cronies installed by Murdoch were capable of executing the business plan. Throughout

1987-88 I observed their efforts with dismay. Sources within Sky were telling me unsettling stories. I told Andrew I thought that Sky was in trouble. He passed the warning to Rupert. We would subsequently both be conscripted to sort it out.

The Luxembourg company Astra had to get its American-made satellite in orbit, and that was a potential show stopper. Launches were not always dependable. No satellite, no Sky. But on the day the satellite was flawlessly launched on top of an Ariane rocket. I was in French Guyana for the *Sunday Times*, flying down on an Air France Concorde with a group of VIPs to see it off. The space base there is the hand of man on the face of God, carved out of Amazonia. The Devil's Island prison where Papillon was confined was just off the coast. My escort warned me about giant poisonous moths. I felt like Tintin looking at the rocket. It was a scene directly from *Destination Moon*. The Tintin resonance was reinforced when the Arianespace team took me to lunch at, wait for it, Chez Tintin. The food was terrific. Grilled prawns with Cayenne peppers. The peppers set me on fire, to the vast amusement of my hosts.

That evening at the space base was literally the hour of the money shot. Murdoch had roughly a billion pounds riding on it. '*Trois-deux-un*', pronounced the French launch director. At the launch control centre I held my breath. But the launch was flawless. The satellite rode the fire to its geostationary parking orbit 35,000km above the equator. I phoned Andrew who phoned Rupert. 'Thank God', he said, Andrew told me later. 'I'm going to pour myself a large drink.' The next day it was farewell to French Guyana. My Concorde broke down in Senegal on the way back to Paris and the Air France crew served us caviar in the Dakar airport cafeteria while they fixed the plane. Senegalese peered through the windows of the cafeteria as the passengers gorged. It was embarrassing.

8

THE BIGGEST GAMBLE

Rupert's Launch of Sky Television—1989
'He who fights monsters should see to it that he himself does not become a
monster'—Friedrich Nietzsche

Shortly after the satellite launch I left the *Sunday Times* and joined
Andrew at Sky. In the hot desk era at Sky headquarters in Isleworth,
I used an office recently vacated by Rupert Murdoch. So naturally I
immediately examined the contents of the waste paper basket to see
what he'd been up to. It was a trick I'd learned at the *Michigan Daily*.
It was revealing.

It was a memo he'd typed himself and had just faxed to the
editor of the *Melbourne Herald*. It was a two-page no-holds-barred
critique of the newspaper's headlines, layout and pictures. As if
Murdoch didn't have enough on his mind, he was bollocking an
editor in Australia on his flaccid journalism.

The satellite launched, Rupert was by now in Master of the
Universe Mode, recklessly biting off more than he could chew. His
tactic was to charge ahead and to spend his way out of trouble.
Rupert is an inveterate gambler and he gambled correctly that he
would be judged by his creditors as too big a debtor to be allowed
to fail.

Murdoch, manic, inhabited an existential time zone. At Sky, he
summoned executive meetings at 7.30 a.m., because he could. He
would bang his fist on the table in the grotty board room of our

headquarters on a grim industrial estate west of London. It was alpha male stuff. But he was razor sharp on the maths, tearing apart the numbers served up.

We were weeks away from the launch of Sky, the dishes and decoders promised by Alan Sugar were late, the Sky News studio wasn't built yet and the forecasts he'd been given by his own Australian cronies didn't add up.

At 57, Murdoch already had a lined, expressive face and every wrinkle quivered as he raged. What he knew and I only suspected was that because of Sky, the Murdoch empire was approaching a financial abyss. We were winning the race to be the first satellite broadcaster on the air, but were haemorrhaging cash. Rupert was dashing back and forth across the Atlantic. He hadn't yet bought his Boeing 737 Business Jet, and still was slumming it on Concorde.

The chattering classes hated the very idea of Sky. Islington, not Isleworth should speak unto the nation, in their opinion. Murdoch's Wapping putsch had infuriated the left, which was still bruised by Mrs Thatcher's muscular defeat of the miners in March 1985. The *Sun*'s uninhibited support for Thatcher infuriated the bien-pensants. The prospect that the BBC-ITV cartel would face ferocious competition from what they imagined would be some kind of SUN TV drove them apoplectic. The consensus clamour from the media establishment was that we should simply be banned. It was a losing argument, as long as Thatcher was prime minister.

It was also an absurd argument because it ignored the fact that even if we went bust, more challengers were just around the corner. A friendly prime minister wouldn't be enough if Sky ran out of cash. Neither would it save the cartel.

The eventual merger later of Sky and the five-channel British Satellite Broadcasting announced in November 1990 was born of necessity because we both were both on the edge of collapse, although we had a real business, and were simply running out of money, and they really didn't have a business and were clueless. After secret negotiations at the Freshfields law firm on Fleet Street (code name Greenacres), a truce was achieved. BSB broke its contract with the Independent Broadcasting Authority and folded its tent. The Sky platform was triumphant. Rupert, after hair-raising brinkmanship with his creditors, persuaded the lenders to roll over the debt. He escaped ignominy but was shaken.

Wot won it was our understanding of the technology. BSB and its IBA sponsor thought that they understood it, but didn't. Our choices meant we launched first. We sold a million dishes before they got out of the gate. Rupert had also smartly calculated the political value of Sky News.[32] The politicians discovered that they liked the idea of more TV exposure. And we had Bart Simpson.

Yes, Sky was the victor on points if not by knockout in the battle with hopeless BSB, an establishment dog that didn't hunt. But Murdoch failed to win the wider war. Rupert later told me that Sky had been his 'greatest achievement as a journalist'. But it turned out to be a Pyrrhic victory.

On the day we launched Sky, this was the prime-time schedule on the four terrestrial TV channels.

BBC One
18:00—Six O'Clock News
18:30—Regional News
19:00—Wogan
20:00—EastEnders
20:30—Screen Two—'The Firm' (Drama)
22:20—Nine O'Clock News
22:50—Crimewatch UK
BBC Two
18:00—Gardeners' World
18:30—The Travel Show
19:00—Newsnight
19:30—Arena—'The Everly Brothers: Songs of Innocence and Experience'
20:30—Bookmark—'Salman Rushdie: The Satanic Verses'
21:30—The Late Show
22:15—Def II—'Rapido'

22:45—The Old Grey Whistle Test
ITV
18:00—News at Six
18:30—Regional News
19:00—Home and Away
19:30—Coronation Street
20:00—Emmerdale Farm
20:30—You Bet!
21:00—The Bill
22:00—News at Ten
22:30—The Ruth Rendell Mysteries
Channel 4
18:00—Channel 4 News
18:55—Fifteen to One
19:30—Brookside
20:00—Equinox—'Time Machine'
21:00—Dispatches
22:00—French and Saunders
22:30—The Comic Strip Presents...—'The Strike'

And that was it. A vast wasteland, for the most part. Some of these programs still exist.

The Sky One launch night schedule looked like this:

18:00—The Sky One Launch Show
18:30—The Simpsons (First Episode)
19:00—Dallas
20:00—The Wonder Years
21:00—The A-Team
22:00—Movie

And it wasn't just Sky One on Astra. Sky News was broadcasting continuous news. There was a movie channel and a sports channel. And proof that ours was an open platform, viewers could also watch MTV, which rode the same satellite. Discovery joined soon after. We had doubled the number of television stations, overnight.

A good argument can be made that less is more, and that more bad television is worse for us than less bad television. On this logic—to which I confess a certain sympathy—it would have been better had television not been invented at all.

But this was not really the choice, the genie was out of the bottle and it was inevitable that broadcasting would change from the paternalistic model established by the regulators to a free for all that would outpace the regulations. Everyone had a TV set, video recorders had appeared, movie rentals were available. The new channels of communication were simply unstoppable and viewers and listeners were going to be liberated, no matter the sneering in the BBC's C-suite.

Rupert's contribution to this revolution was enormous. He kicked down the door and others followed. But he would ultimately lose control of his own creation. His share of the market would shrink. From feared media tycoon he would become just another player, a lion in winter. Murdoch opened British television to competition, but ultimately lost Sky to Comcast and the internet to the tech bros.

And now a new satellite revolution is coming. Satellites have continued to evolve with growing constellations in low-earth orbit, like Elon Musk's SpaceX starlink system, capable of communicating directly with mobile devices. The satellite we used to launch Sky is long out of service. Fibre optics and internet streaming are the future, not his newspapers or his television stations.

9

MAKING MISCHIEF

Freedom in broadcasting, for or against?—1988

Arriving at 10 Downing Street on a damp evening in late 1988, the door opens magically. I wait a minute in the lobby with a policeman who has an antique revolver, then am collected by a functionary and escorted to the office of Brian Griffith, a razor sharp economist, the head of Prime Minister Margaret Thatcher's policy unit. The product of the Dynevor Secondary Grammar School in Swansea, he was one of the intellectual engines behind the phenomenon of Thatcherism. He was subsequently ennobled as Baron Griffiths of Fforestfach. I last ran into him at Windsor Castle, with Prince Andrew, of all people.

Number 10 has subsequently been modernised but then it was a ramshackle building, practically Dickensian. There were no computers, obviously. The interior was exactly the exhausted esthetic of *Yes, Prime Minister*. The leaderene was not one for lavishing money on interiors. William Gladstone might have popped around the corner at any moment. Margaret had told Rupert to go full ahead with the Sky project, and Brian and I were to work out the details. I accepted a whisky (although Diet Coke was then my usual tipple) and we talked satellites. He was keenly interested in the technology and the potential for competition. Reforming the BBC was proving impossible, he told me.

Margaret Thatcher put her head around the door and noticing

me in the visitor's chair, apologised for interrupting and said she would see him later.

Elon Musk is today's bogeyman but in 1989 it was Murdoch, intensely disliked because he was a foreigner (Australian and worse also a naturalised American), he had too-ruthlessly cut off the print unions at the knees (not a British thing to do), was generally disruptive of the established order and most unforgivable of all, unequivocally supported Thatcher, who supported him in return. They were both under siege.

Not only was Sky on the edge of a financial catastrophe, but there was pressure in Whitehall and Westminster to intervene to stop us, lest the country's supposedly delicate media ecology be disrupted. I had sent Brian our manifesto, *Freedom in Broadcasting: For or against?* I wrote it with Irwin Stelzer, a super-smart economist and confidant of Murdoch who had been parachuted in from New York. Brian had read it and was 100% on board. He promised me unequivocally that Downing Street had our back. The efforts to stop us were outrageous, he opined. She wasn't going to let anyone stop us, he promised. Message received.

If the British establishment didn't like Murdoch, the feeling was mutual. Murdoch held the London chattering classes in contempt. Some of this animus he had inherited from his father Sir Keith Murdoch, who had exposed Pom incompetence in the disastrous Gallipoli operation during the Great War. The rest is attributable to the chip on Rupert's own shoulder.

Rupert had attended Oxford, given it money, and thought he had ticked the boxes for acceptance in Britain. But he complained that despite his support for the unprofitable *Times* and his courageous showdown with the unions, which liberated every other publisher, when he came to Britain, he was made to feel unwelcome. This is why he finally embraced America, where the elite establishment accepted him as a member.

Murdoch had real enemies. In Britain, the usual nabobs—unions, academics, the BBC, the *Guardian* newspaper, the Labour Party, Islington snobs—were perpetually and petulantly outraged at every move he made. The Murdoch hysteria was being energetically whipped up by BSB, which was still in business, and its powerful media industry backers.[33] They were out to get him simply because their business plan had overlooked the possibility of competition. His *Sun* newspaper was bad enough. That Murdoch should make a move on the British television industry was too much. They tried very hard to stop him.

It was my task to advocate for the devil and so I opened an office in Westminster and schmoozed Whitehall. I'd been on the receiving end of PR but this was my first go at the dark art. My message was to rebrand bad Rupert as good Rupert, the saviour of free broadcasting in Britain. A tough sell.

I wasn't a natural lobbyist merely a seconded journalist so I made it up. I had an actor dress up as a character from our surprise hit show and invited MPs for drinks at my war room on Victoria Street. Which was less a war room than a shabby suite of offices in a building soon to be torn down. I ordered a lot of drinks because many honourable members came and many were thirsty. John Bercow was greasing his way around the room. Later Speaker of the House of Commons he had been seconded to my team from the lobbying firm we hired. He was a sneaky character even then and a professed right-wing Thatcherite, until he later wasn't. I'm not recalling that he added a lot of value as he spent much of his time looking for a safe parliamentary seat, but he did his share of schmoozing for Rupert.

Our offices on Victoria Street were opposite New Scotland Yard where not much seemed to be happening, as far as I could tell. I maintained surveillance on police HQ by instinct. I'd started as a police reporter, after all. But everyone at Scotland Yard seemed to rush home at five o'clock. The lights were on but nobody was at home. Our side of Victoria Street was however seething with conspiracy, and not just my own conspiracies to make Rupert loved and discredit our opponents. Lord Heseltine and Michael Mates had offices upstairs, where they were openly plotting the downfall of Mrs Thatcher. Many treasonous Tory MPs snuck in and out. The shifty plotters avoided eye contact with me in the lift. Margaret's days were numbered. She resigned on November 28, 1990, but she hung on long enough for us.

Our enemies were making mischief against us and I was making mischief of my own. I snuck Norman Tebbit into the Labour Party conference in Brighton, to the fury of Peter Mandelson, to record a show called Target with Austin Mitchell, a journalist, the famously maverick Labour MP for Grimsby. It was great TV, modelled on the American show Crossfire with Michael Kinsley at his most acerbic and wicked (of whom more later) and Pat Buchanan, a pugnacious conservative polemist and speechwriter for Ronald Reagan, who ran three times for the presidency. Tebbit and Mitchell offered chemistry just as good. Does civil and clever debate exist on news channels anymore? It was a big win to have pictures of Norman Tebbit in the papers the next day. And as a bonus of course Mandelson had a tantrum. That was very satisfying. He was cruising for a bruising and confronted the Sky team as we were leaving the convention centre, screaming, 'get him out of here.' How we laughed. Norman was great fun but would be instantly cancelled today. I spent a lot of time with Tebbit and Mitchell. When we were discussing Norman Baker's half-baked dangerous dogs bill backstage one day, he advanced his opinion that the solution to dangerous dogs was immigration from Korea. Austin was a member of the almost-disappeared species of libertarian socialists and didn't even pretend to defend the most absurd shibboleths of his own party.

BSB was so inept that making trouble for them was largely unnecessary but I poured salt in the wounds whenever possible. I tracked down the inventor of BSB's promised squarial satellite antenna and discovered it wouldn't work and there was nobody to make it. I wrote pro-Sky speeches for MPs and members of the House of Lords and gleefully read my own words in Hansard.

The argument of the chattering classes was that allowing Murdoch to operate TV stations would give him excess power in the media industry because of his cross-ownership of newspapers. They claimed that Murdoch 'controlled' the newspaper market. And that with a four-channel television bouquet offering a news channel, sports channel, movie channel and general entertainment channel, he would use cross-promotion to also control the TV market.

It was a ridiculous argument considering that Murdoch would have to build his network one house at a time, while the existing duopoly had access to every home. I took Rupert to meetings in the Palace of Westminster to meet friendly MPs and peers.

Ours was a manifesto for freedom underpinned by solid arguments. So what if it was true that Murdoch had a 40% share of the newspaper market, between *The Times*, the *Sun*, the *Sunday Times* and the *News of the World*? This wasn't control, it was entirely due to the choices made by readers. Nobody forced anyone to buy his newspapers. And there were plenty of alternatives. Murdoch was merely acutely tuned in to his customers. They loved his papers, especially the *Sun*.

Andrew Neil's book, *Full Disclosure* (1996) is the definitive account of Sky's launch but he missed a crucial angle. Bart Simpson's name doesn't appear in the index. To my mind, he was the saviour of Murdoch. Or, at the very least, the argument can be made. Our programming was pretty ropey otherwise. An American show called 21 Jump Street was our headline show. It never really caught on. Rupert himself was contemptuous of it, referring to its star Johnny Depp as 'that faggot'.

The Simpsons were the *deus ex machina* and why Sky still exists. The show became a cultural phenomenon, misinterpreted widely as the story of a dysfunctional family but in fact, quite the opposite. The Simpsons have always stayed together. The show is still going a quarter century later but has lost its magic.

When I took the first Simpsons tapes home, before the launch, and showed them to my kids, I knew we'd win the battle against British Satellite Broadcasting. We owned the zeitgeist. BSB could eat our shorts. The Simpsons was ubiquitous in 1989, boosted not least by our shameless cross-promotion in the *Sun*, the ubiquity of Simpsons toys, t-shirts and tittle-tattle. Everyone loved the show, including, importantly, the children of Tory big wigs. Bart probably did more to save Sky than any of us.

10

CAMDEN LOCK

A Discovery—1991
A person with a new idea is a crank until the idea succeeds—Mark Twain.

I could almost title this part of the story, 'how I got my Virgin Atlantic gold card', so frequent became my crossing of the herring pond, in my ultimately failed mission to explain the potential of the internet to News Corporation. By 1991 Sky (having absorbed rival BSB) was moving forward at pace, the make-mischief brief was over and the internet was not understood at all. I was parachuted back into Wapping, where a grown-up chief executive had been put in charge at the insistence of Murdoch's creditors, who wanted discipline and bondage. Gus Fischer, a Swiss safe pair of hands, was installed in the big office opposite Andrew Knight, who was nominally chairman but didn't do much. I liked Gus a lot, too much ultimately because when he was corporately assassinated, I had attached myself too closely to his coat-tails and eventually became collateral damage.

But first I was given an office on the top floor of the Wapping complex and saw all the comings and goings in the C-suite.

We were on a charm offensive after the print strike had been settled with the unions surrendering and Sky's future assured in the new joint venture with BSB. I thought we should make friends with some of the Labour MPs who had recently been howling for us to be put out of business. A reset seemed prudent.

Diane Abbot came to lunch and was funny and clever. She has subsequently had a difficult time, especially with her son and her health. I introduced her to Kelvin MacKenzie, the irascible editor of the *Sun*, and she asked him to show her the Prince Andrew willie pictures, then a talking point, which he hadn't published, but were in a drawer of his desk. She wept with laughter.

Other than have people to lunch, there wasn't a tremendous amount for me to do. I adored my boss, Jane Reed, the head of corporate affairs, and the former editor of the great *Women's Own*, but there were no great battles to be fought, only skirmishes. I was sent to Berlin after the Wall came down, because Rupert had the idea of launching a version of The Sun, aimed at east Germans. It didn't work out. Jane and I went to the EU 'Assises' on the press in Brussels, which was a horror story with EU bureaucrats trying to extend their benevolent regulation upon us. I was very rude to them. I pointed out that in Britain we had a thriving, competitive newspaper market and intervention from Brussels wasn't welcome. This all became academic after Brexit. But it was too quiet a life and I'd been away from journalism too long, since my secondment from the *Sunday Times* to Sky. So I returned to the *Sunday Times* with a column and the title of Assistant Editor, which didn't mean much except I got to attend most of the important meetings, including the story conference at which the section editors would produce their proposals for the next week's newspaper.

Andrew had already been expelled from the tent, sent to New York to develop a show for Fox. The new editor was John Witherow, a talented journalist and former foreign editor. We got on well. He was contrarian, had been foreign editor, hence was wise to the world, and liked amusing stories, which were part of my repertoire. Sending executives to New York, it turned out, was equivalent to being sent to the departure lounge, as Andrew was to discover then, and I was to discover later.

Other than writing a column, and drafting the paper's Leader,[34] I still didn't really have a lot to do, so to make it appear that I was worth what had become a gratifying salary, I bought an Apple

Macintosh computer in 1992 and began to explore the nascent internet. Mrs Miller accused me of wasting money. Quickly I was sure it would become the next big thing, although I couldn't imagine how big.

Everybody already had an Atex terminal but I was the first in Wapping with a computer on my desk that was connected to the world. All the other terminals could do no more than send copy to the subs and the typesetter in the basement. I have been on some wild adventures but those early days of the internet were a revelation. Or perhaps not so much a revelation, because it was absolutely unclear what it meant, as an epiphany. The difference between I get it, and wow. I don't suppose this was especially insightful. Much of the population of the planet has subsequently had a similar Stephen Dedalus moment. I suspect, however, that I was among the first, and among very few journalists, to begin to understand how this was going to change everything.

The amount of time I was spending online was a harbinger of the forthcoming global time suck. Because let no-one doubt that this is what it has become. Wherever I go in the world now, everyone has their phone to their face.

The story of the Internet has never been definitively told and cannot be because it is so atomised and the critical mass so incomprehensible. We can only reconstruct the origins through our personal experiences. There was an innocence and pioneer spirit to the community of those probing the new digital world. Also a naive belief that this beautiful thing would never be controlled by evil forces. The internet would interpret censorship as damage, and route around it—at least that was the idea.

I soon hooked up with two of the first online message boards, The Well in San Francisco and CIX, in Woking, Surrey. What we chatted about, mainly, was the internet. Only one other journalist at Wapping shared my fascination, John Diamond, then married to Nigella Lawson. John had started a *Times* discussion group on CIX and had the idea of harvesting the best comments from the online world and printing them in the newspaper. John was to die not long afterwards and his brilliant idea died with him.

I was convinced that whatever the internet might become, News Corporation should be part of it and should defend its market position on this new terrain. I took my laptop up to the executive floor at Wapping to show Gus Fischer what I was discovering. His patronage was to lead me to a new adventure, where I witnessed Murdoch at his worst.

Fischer's relationship with Murdoch was fraught. The lenders had demanded grown-up management and Murdoch reluctantly hired Fischer to appease them. Until Murdoch was ultimately able to terminate Fischer, he had referred to Wapping as 'enemy occupied territory'. But Murdoch was preoccupied with America, and so for a while Fischer had lots of autonomy. I didn't see that Fischer was a dead man walking and threw in my lot with him.

He was a very smart guy and 'got it' immediately when I showed him what I was discovering, including the very earliest American newspaper experiments going online. I was not sure what any of this might mean. The *Columbus Dispatch* in Ohio had experimented putting up articles on Compuserve, an early American online service. Why not *The Times*? I suggested setting up an internet lab.

He didn't hesitate. There was no business plan or spreadsheet. He told me to go see Stephen Kirk, who had set up a News Corporation affiliate in Camden Town offering wildly profitable telephone-based competitions to readers of the *Sun*. Kirk was a mystical character, into Kaballah and a friend of Yuri Geller. He entertained eccentric beliefs, e.g. that nuclear fusion would be possible, if only we believed in it, and he had a levitation room in his house.

He was also a sharp and creative businessman. He was coining money and open to new ideas that weren't particularly appealing to the newspaper culture in Wapping. Fischer kept him well away from Murdoch.

I went to see Stephen, who was occupying a magnificent brick beer warehouse converted into open-plan offices, named the Elephant House. It was next to the TV-am studios at Camden Lock and originally a bottle store for the Camden Brewery. It featured a prominent elephant's head on the building, a tribute to Elephant Pale Ale. It was altogether a funky venue to launch a new media lab.

Kirk offered me the top floor of his building to create my new playpen. Camden Lock became Silicon Lock. I hired half a dozen lovable geeky students from UCL and we were off. I don't know how Gus and Stephen did it, but we ordered computers and phone lines and the purchase orders flew. Within weeks we had launched a website titled Camden Lock using the new World Wide Web to serve content to the growing community of internet users in Britain and around the world.

The *New Yorker* had recently run a cartoon showing a dog sitting by a computer captioned, 'On the internet nobody knows you're a dog.' We immediately gave an email address to my dog Sam and published a webpage of his daily walks on Hampstead Heath. The UCL students were super creative and pre-woke. One of my girl geeks decided to get a nipple pierced at a local tattoo parlour. On the theory that if the *Sun* did nipples, so could we, we did a story with no graphic detail spared. We were prophets without profit. My team came up with the idea of publishing videos, sent in by users. This was five years before YouTube. We made an interactive video game with its own internal daily newspaper and had it running 10 years before such games became common. In my naivety I thought Rupert would eventually notice this and proclaim me a genius and master of all things digital, but this was not to be what happened as we were soon razed to dust.

That there was not much native understanding of the internet amongst Rupert's editors was not surprising. But their inability to even process the existence of the internet was a little shocking. I went to see Peter Stothard, then the editor of *The Times*, to convince him that we could publish his newspaper online. I told him that not only could we distribute *The Times*, but that it could be constantly updated during the day. I was too enthusiastic. He was decidedly unimpressed. 'I don't want to do that', he said. 'Here, we reflect on the news,' he added. He, nevertheless, allowed me to tap into his data and *The Times* became the first newspaper in Britain with an online presence. It was crude text only that Wapping could supply and the *Daily Telegraph* soon outdid us with a web browser version of itself but at least we were in the game.

I was keen to push this, publish all of our papers online, and develop Camden Lock as an entirely novel online service for students and young people. This was where my disruptive instincts collided with my corporate naivety. I failed to read the boardroom.

In America, Rupert had started making moves of his own, although all of them were crazy. While we were getting on with it in London, he rashly bought Delphi Internet Services, a dull computer services company in Cambridge, Massachussetts, which had mainly been serving porn using a pre-Web protocol called Newsnet. He imagined this would somehow get him onto the information superhighway. He then put a relative of his wife, who needed a job, in charge of it. Delphi sent a man to London to spy on us. He came and went. I came and went in the other direction, to spy on Delphi. Rupert hired McKinsey who came to see what we were doing. That cost $1 million, apparently. None of my encounters with McKinsey have enabled me to understand this company's success.

Murdoch then did an absurd deal with the MCI telecommunications company, a company even duller than Delphi, an operator of long-distance telephone services. The blind were leading the blind. The plan was to start a brand new internet company, to be called the I-Guide, to be based in New York City, which was to feature human editors curating the internet, as if it was in the power of humans to do so. Altavista and Google were soon to demonstrate this, indexing the totality of the internet in real time, and serving users interactively. Murdoch thought of the I-Guide like *TV Guide* magazine, which he now owned, except that instead of being a guide to television, it would be a guide for the internet. This was bonkers. The internet was infinite but Murdoch seemed to think it was something fixed, like the number of TV stations in Little Rock. He then hired the editor of *TV Guide,* Anthea Disney, a former Daily Mail journalist, to run it. She then hired her husband to be picture editor.

This simply wasn't serious.

It was chaos in the temporary I-Guide office at News Corporation headquarters at 1211 Avenue of the Americas and nothing was getting done because everyone was in meetings. This wasn't move-fast-and-break-things. It was infighting for a larger slice of corporate pie.

Then Murdoch fired Gus Fischer and things got really crazy.

If I were to be fair and balanced, I would say that what I saw was not at all unique; all great media companies fumbled and dithered their way online. But the Murdoch fumble and dither and failure was the one I experienced and it was epic.

It was decreed that a floor of a gigantic downtown building was to be fitted out for the launch of the I-Guide. Downtown was supposed to represent the new attitude to new media.

I was sent to the scene supposedly as some sort of senior editor if not the editor, it was never clear, until the former *TV Guide* editor arrived. I found dozens of producers had been hired but it wasn't at all clear what anyone was supposed to do. Gigantic investments were being made in a data centre in Cambridge and colossally expensive software had been purchased with no apparent utility. Many staffers were hired to do the same job. Although the nature of the job for which they were hired was never made entirely clear. There were signing bonuses and housing allowances. Money was burned to execute Murdoch's unachievable vision. I was being extremely well paid to have a ringside seat and no influence whatsoever.

There was an incineration of at least $200 million before News Corporation and MCI pulled the plug, with nothing to show for the effort. Camden Lock in London where my brainy geeks were inventing the future and who could have developed products worth maybe billions, and where I'd spent 100th of that sum, was brutally destroyed in the aftermath. My year of commuting across the Atlantic trying to save this was completely wasted.

I was summoned to a meeting with two Australian Murdoch cronies sent to recapture Wapping. It was a disaster. Brutal. I wanted to convince the temporary new management that London should have some autonomy, and seize the giant business opportunities. I argued that our share of this new digital space should be at least as large as it was in print. I said we should buy CIX, a tiny startup internet provider in Surbiton, so we could scale our servers. No, no, no, no, no.

They weren't interested. Indeed they were contemptuous. They announced at the beginning of our first and only meeting that my idea for a studio creating web pages for our group and beyond was a non-starter because soon everyone who wanted a web page would have one, and that would be that.

I set up a projector and gave them a course in internet 101, showing them how with a click, a user could skip around the net. Stupidly, I demonstrated this by clicking between wacky Camden Lock, our rolling web log with its nipple piercing and dog walks, and *The Times*. The Australians were clueless and horrified. They accused me of devaluing *The Times* by associating it with groovy Camden Lock, just one click away. Practically pornography, they declared, a few hundred feet away from where the *Sun*'s picture editor was selecting the next day's sizzler. They were unable to grasp that on the internet, everything is one click away.

The monumental stupidity of these executives was breathtaking and insurmountable. The kindest interpretation is that they were acting on orders from New York, to burn down anything Gus had created.

Camden Lock was shut down and every trace of its existence was wiped clean. My geeks have gone on to make fortunes, I hope. Murdoch continued to flounder. In July 2005 he bought the social network MySpace for $580 million. It was crushed by Facebook and he subsequently sold it for $35 million. It's subsequently taken years for News Corporation to come to terms with the internet as an also ran.

11

FIRED

Almost everyone gets sacked in the end—1989

Getting fired by Rupert may have been the best thing that ever happened to me. It was inevitable and desirable. Although later I turned out to have been only semi-fired, as I was re-admitted to the bosom of the *Sunday Times* as a columnist. It was a soft landing and life got much more interesting. I had been released from the force field of a Jekyll and Hyde character capable of swinging from charmer to monster, who was making terrible decisions.

Although Murdoch World was quite the spectacle, I could not have stayed longer without becoming something I'm not. But I won't deny it was a wild ride, and a spectacle. I wouldn't claim to have been a super intimate confidante of the boss, but I saw a lot. So from the wreckage of my career at News Corporation, I at least had a good story. I'd seen the human dynamo/ visionary/ charmer/ gambler/ monster close up. There's a sequel to Citizen Kane, right there, if I can ever write the screenplay. There's plenty of colour. For a while, I saw a lot of him. Not just at the office. There was a *Sunday Times* dinner at his flat overlooking Green Park, the first of my chow downs with the boss. He sipped white wine and beamed. We were making a profit of £1 million a week. Then there was dinner with him and Irwin Stelzer at Andrew Neil's flat in South Kensington, where we had a pow-wow how to counter the campaign against us. He was all business, but stressed, weighed down by financial pressures. And my one-on-one lunch at the commissary at the 20th Century Fox lot in Los Angeles, the summit and inevitable descent of my career at News Corporation, about which more later.

I'd seen him going broke, on the verge of humiliation. And watched him bluff his way through questions about his financial position. I had even put words in his mouth. I flew up to Edinburgh with him where he gave a speech at the Television Festival in 1989. We had a meeting with him in his grotty hotel room to rehearse the speech. Murdoch duly performed before a hostile audience at McEwan Hall. Written by Andrew Neil, Irwin Stelzer and me, the speech was a tendentious affair. It attacked the narrow elite that believed it had the right to impose its values on viewers. I sat in the auditorium amidst the squirming elite under attack.

But there was always the vibe that this would come to an end, and such an end can be abrupt, in Murdochland. Very few 'retired' from the court of Murdoch to collect a gold watch. I was briefly a golden boy, but didn't even get a thank you. When my number came up I was in New York and when I got the call for a meeting with HR, I wasn't surprised.

It was tedious with the lawyers but we got the separation done and promised not to disparage one another. The payoff was generous, a year's salary, which was by then substantial.

Because I am generous-minded, I admit it was partly my fault that we parted company. I'm not a natural company man. But it wasn't entirely my fault. Rupert was screwing up the internet, which I was certain was the future. I was pissed off. Our stars weren't aligning. I hadn't much liked what I'd been seeing in New York. He had some formidably mediocre people working for him and since I've never bitten my tongue I said so. I made more mischief than was wise and my loyalty knew its limits.

Rupert had by this point started heading into the disagreeable, manic, narcissistic behaviour that is a pathology common with press and media tycoons. Not only was he obnoxious but he wasn't even doing a good job running the parts of the company that I could see. He had sacked Gus Fischer, who was competent, whom I'd liked and who'd looked after me. He'd destroyed my brilliant start-up at the Elephant House in Camden Town pursuing a daft and doomed venture with a clueless telephone company. News Corporation headquarters on the Avenue of the Americas in New York was stuffed with highly paid people who apparently did nothing at all except attend meetings. 'What's your job?' I demanded of one suit. 'Liaison and coordination', was the unconvincing answer.

The exception to this corporate malaise was Fox News, the fiefdom of Roger Ailes.[35] That's because Ailes fought tooth and nail to stop Murdoch and his cronies from buggering up what became a gigantic success and the number one news channel in America. Murdoch ultimately fired him. Ailes died soon after.

Murdoch's catastrophic personal life and divorce settlement with Anna Torv is now setting up an epic battle for the future of News Corporation, diminished but still a global enterprise that controls Fox News, the *Wall Street Journal*, the *New York Post*, HarperCollins, and a large collection of newspapers and television outlets in Australia and Britain including *The Times*, *Sunday Times* and *Sun*. Anna filed for divorce in California, a community-property state, where she was entitled to half of everything built since their marriage 31 years earlier.

She sacrificed that right during the divorce negotiations to ensure that Rupert's four existing children—and not any future heirs—would inherit his fortune after his death. It is denied that the television drama Succession was based on the Murdoch clan, but the only difference is that the Murdoch succession is even more complicated, with six not three children in the fight. Murdoch has attempted, unsuccessfully so far, to unwind his settlement with Anna in a Nevada court. He's running out of time, to be blunt.

The Murdoch succession battle has raged for decades[36] and isn't over, even if he wins a legal round or two. The kids have fought tooth and nail. Of his sons from his marriage to Anna Torv, it was the eldest, Lachlan, who was eventually designated to take over, vanquishing his sibling James. Neither would ever have been put in charge in a more normal business, but News Corporation is a family affair. Lachlan was chosen because Rupert thinks he is the only one of his children who will prevent the empire from falling into the hands of the progressives in his own family. Whether his solution proves durable remains to be seen.

Lachlan's most notable independent business foray before joining the family firm was a doomed joint venture with James Packer, the son of Kerry Packer, another Australian tycoon and a companion of Murdoch père at gambling tables in Las Vegas. One.Tel, their telecommunications company, collapsed in 2001, losing $1 billion. Lachlan bears only a vague resemblance to Kendall Roy in the TV show. He's not as smart as he thinks he is, but also not drug-addled.

Son number two James, currently exiled and in exquisite rebellion against the old man, has become a progressive activist. I remember him standing outside the Royal Institution in London where he admired an Aston Martin and pretended he couldn't afford one. There's some resonance with Roman Roy with his impulsive behaviour. Murdoch has been so determined to protect the political legacy of his media empire, particularly Fox News, that he has sought to exclude James and stop him mounting a coup against his brother. James is unlikely to consider himself out of the game, once his father exits.

The smart daughter, Elisabeth, the inspiration for Shiv Roy in the TV show, has gone her own way and built a successful television production business, which she then sold to her father for a generous price, making a profit of more than £150 million. She was once married to Matthew Freud. But she's not happy with Lachlan's status. Neither is her half-sister Prudence. Prue is also a progressive. Murdoch's children from other marriages are theoretically out of the succession loop but his daughters by Wendy Deng, Grace, 23, and Chloe, 21, are staking claims, too.

The bottom line is that News Corporation is eternally brutal and with the death of Murdoch might well disintegrate.

I won't be present at the fall. I abandoned the brownstone they paid for in Gramercy Park and returned, unemployed, to London, where we bought a house in Hampstead, the purchase lubricated with the payoff. I flew back in Upper Class, just as a final C-suite gesture.

12

THE EUROPEAN

And My Role in its Downfall—1996

In London again, unemployed, again. Senior Management (Mrs Miller) tolerated my indolence only briefly before instructing me to get a job. It was my luck that following his own separation from the court of Murdoch, Andrew Neil was at the *European* newspaper, newly acquired by the extremely odd Barclay brothers, whose story is a book on its own.[37]

Andrew was gallantly trying to flog a dying horse. Founded by Robert Maxwell, the corpulent proprietor of Mirror Group Newspapers, the *European* was created by him as 'Europe's first national newspaper' at a time when newspapers were about to crash and burn. Maxwell failed with the title, and then died in mysterious circumstances. He was a deeply unpleasant man with a dubious past. Fair to say we didn't get on. Once he telephoned me at the *Sunday Times* after I had written a rude story about him and he told me, 'Why don't you just fuck off.' After his death it was revealed that he had embezzled hundreds of millions of pounds from the *Mirror*'s pension fund to prop up his struggling empire. I suppose it is a badge of honour that he hated me.

The European then fell into the hands of the Barclay twins, who were building a media portfolio that would eventually include the *Daily Telegraph*, *Sunday Telegraph* and *Spectator*. Aidan Barclay, the son of Sir David, had ambitions to launch new publications and hired

Andrew. The *European* was now housed in splendid quarters on the top floor of the ITN building on Gray's Inn Road.

Andrew offered me an office with a view, a generous salary, and the title of business editor, which was a bit of a stretch as I was never a financial journalist. We brewed up some good stories at the paper but our errors were fundamental. This was a Bataan death march. Our line—pro-Europe, EU sceptical—was intellectually sound but didn't find much of an audience. But the problem was worse than that. We were trying to do the last thing we'd done, which was to produce a newspaper on paper. This was not rational as print was about to blow up. Print wasn't quite dead yet. But it was entering the death spiral.

The European was doomed, but it was fun while it lasted. The offices were terrific and modern. There were plenty of places to eat in the neighbourhood. There seemed to be plenty of money. We had solid journalists on staff including Peter Millar and Paula Hawkins, who subsequently abandoned journalism to be a novelist and made millions with *The Girl on the Train*.

The *European* finally collapsed in 1998, to become just another forgotten tombstone in the graveyard of print. The original sin was the idealistic vision of Maxwell for a common European newspaper. It was a poisoned concept to the roots. The most fundamental problem was that it was a newspaper. Despite heroic efforts attempting to reposition the paper as a high-end tabloid rival to the *Economist*, success eluded us.

Our online efforts were feeble. It was possible to download pdfs of the print edition. That was it. Our entire attitude was inconsistent with the zeitgeist. Andrew and I should have known better. The political line was unsustainable. We had both spent time grappling with Brussels when we were at Sky and the *Sunday Times*. We were hugely cynical about the EU. This put the paper in an impossibly conflicted position. We were perceived as anti-European, although we really weren't. Our approach was never going to fly. We loved Europe and free trade. We were just sceptical of the grand designs of the official European project. We published some decent journalism but nobody was paying attention.

13

WAR

Is this Ishmaelia? No, Kukes—1999

When I was at Bedales School, my history teacher Ruth Whiting, in her signature green ink, scrawled on the bottom of one of my essays the single word, 'journalese'. She meant it as an insult. I took it as career advice. I didn't learn much else there. *Pace* Mark Twain, I never let schooling interfere with my education.

I hid in the wonderful, oaken Bedales Library, an Arts and Crafts masterpiece and a place of dreams for me. The librarian, Gonda Stamford, a refugee from Nazi Germany, put me in charge of the history and economics stacks. But it was on the fiction shelves that I discovered the best book ever written about journalism, *Scoop*, by Evelyn Waugh, about the adventures of the country life columnist turned accidental war correspondent, William Boot, of the *Daily Beast*, a newspaper with an uncanny resemblance to the *Daily Express*. Waugh based the story of a war in the fictional African nation of Ishmaelia on his own experiences as a *Daily Mail* correspondent in Africa in 1935, during the Italian-Abyssinian war. *Scoop* is the essential book on war reporting, which was something I'd always wanted to try. I was too young to be a journalist in Vietnam. And now suddenly I had my chance.

When I went to Kosovo as a mid-life debutant war reporter, after my misadventures with Rupert Murdoch, I was keen to cross the Boot of the *Beast* fantasy off my bucket list, I discovered the novel was essentially true. Albania was almost precisely like Ishmaelia in Waugh's novel. Redolent, at least. Most of the time, we journalists had no clue what was going on.

The war had attracted many spectators, as it was easy to get to from Italy by hydrofoil or by air from Slovenia to the Mother Teresa Airport outside Tirana.

Among the many war tourists of unexplained affiliation were mysterious journalists who disappeared for days at a time before emerging with improbable scoops. The weary seen-it-all veterans were hanging out at the hotel bar. I discovered Jeremy Bowen by the pool of the Rogner hotel, the most expensive in Tirana, largely occupied by the BBC. And then there was me, miles out of my depth.

In the old days Reuters special correspondents were told that the first priority upon arriving in a conflict zone was to locate the telegraph office. But instead of a telegraph office, which played a central role in *Scoop*, there was an internet café, which functioned when there was power, which was sometimes.[38]

It was a shock to the system, going to a war, even if it was rather a small war, and I was a fairly useless war correspondent, but it was the only war I have seen and I'm glad I went. I don't need to see another one.

How did I find myself in Kosovo? It was 1999, I was 48, and if I didn't quite go to war by accident, like Boot, it was certainly an unexpected event. At the time a focus of my *Sunday Times* journalism was a futile effort to debunk the millennium bug story. It was a gigantically profitable hoax, and was enabled by an ignorant media. It was a good story and John Witherow let me write about it but I was generally ignored even by the *Sunday Times* which allowed me to express dissidence in my column but otherwise went along with the nonsense, which was tantalising and exciting whereas I was just selling the line, 'don't panic'. I couldn't compete with wild tales of nuclear power stations that might spontaneously combust and planes falling out of the sky. I asked Anthony Finklestein, the head of the computer department at University College, London, later knighted, if I was wrong. No, he said, it was a scam. Were we facing the end of civilisation? No. Was the media coverage hysterical? Yes. Would he go on the record? Absolutely not. Too many of his colleagues were making big money from it. And my media colleagues weren't doing too badly, either.

I was boring Britain, flogging the unexciting truth about the millennium bug, when Merrill Brown, the editor at the new MSNBC joint venture between NBC News and Microsoft,[39] called me out of the blue from New York. I had known Merrill in Washington when he was a business reporter for the *Washington Post* and he used to call me to pump me for stories. Now he had become a big enchilada and in remembrance of plots passé, asked me if I would be interested in going to Albania.

Tomorrow. To cover the conflict provoked by Serbian expulsions of ethnic Albanians from Kosovo. The refugees were crossing the frontier to Albania in the northern highlands. It was very telegenic, very tense and the job paid $500 a day, which seemed a lot at the time.

Brown wanted to know, before sealing the deal, did I know what I was doing, going to a war? Of course I did, I lied. No worries. I'd been a police reporter in the war zone of Detroit, I told myself. How could this be much different?

So I bought some stout boots (no cleft sticks for messengers, like Boot of the Beast—I had a rudimentary satellite telephone) and flew to Bari, in southern Italy. I caught the hydrofoil to Albania the next morning. I don't know the collective noun for war correspondents—a press, a scoop, a hack?—but there was barely anyone else but journalists on the ferry, other than some toughs keeping to themselves, whom I now conjecture, in the light of subsequent understanding, to have been gangsters.

We docked at Durrës, the dusty main sea port of Albania. Much passing of dollars occurred as the customs men feasted on bribes that could be harvested from passing the mountain of television equipment. I got off lightly, bribing a customs man with $10 to return my 'disappeared' passport. Bribes in Albania were good value for money at the time.

The ITN crew offered me a ride 150km north to the scene of the action. They had a driver with a new long-wheel-base Land Rover, the property of a Canadian mining company that had just abandoned the country. It was a solid vehicle but the road with steep ravines, crumbling surfaces and no guard rails was more terrifying than anything I have seen before or since and more frightening by far than any of the subsequent random thumps, bangs and puffs of distant smoke in the conflict zone. It was soon dusk and the driver was navigating with headlights. Perhaps I would die before even getting to the war.

Merrill had told me that after getting to Albania I should head to the town of Kukes in the north, next to the Serbian/Kosovo border. I should go to the bar-hotel Adria, which had been commandeered by NBC. I should hook up with their team and take it from there.

Kukes had been invaded by scores of Western journalists and many had established their headquarters at the Bar America. Roast animal head was the specialty of the kitchen. It was an analogue of the Hotel Liberty in *Scoop*, where the journalists huddled together, keeping an eye on one another. The Bar America was heaving late into the night. The journalists dressed up in warry outfits with those photographer jackets with lots of pockets for all the bits and pieces, and your blood group written on it with a sharpie. The Bar America was the last place I saw the *Sunday Times's* Marie Colvin, who was subsequently killed in Homs.

One difference from the Waugh book is that a lot of war correspondents were now women. In *Scoop* there are significant women, principally Julia Stitch, inspired by Lady Diana Cooper. She sets the plot in motion by arranging for a John Courtney Boot to be sent as a journalist to Africa, but due to a mix-up, William Boot, the *Beast's* nature columnist, is instead summoned to depart for war. Katchen, a femme fatale, manipulates Boot during his time in Ishmaelia, using him for her own gain. But there are no women journalists in *Scoop*.

I made my way to the Adria, on a side street. It would be generous to call this establishment a hotel. The plumbing was primitive, the heating system inadequate and the nights intensely cold. Outside on the pavement sacks of American USAID flour marked 'not for sale' were being hawked by men in leather jackets, carrying pistols. The Albanian currency was ignored, everything was priced in dollars.

The bar of the Adria summarised the contradictions. An illuminated verse of the Koran was displayed behind the bar next to a prized bottle of Scotch whisky. Under the counter the bartender kept an AK-47 assault rifle. These guns were everywhere in Albania, after the looting of the armouries after the fall of the communist regime. Some were Russian, some Chinese but the Albanians favoured the Czech ones.

At our squalor pit a second NBC crew had just arrived after driving in overland from Montenegro. They brought beer and bravado. There was much fantabulism as the crews told their war stories. They weren't on a mission to bring the horror of war home to American living rooms but because it was fun and they were making fantastic amounts of money.

The scene at the Adria was now cinematic. Hundreds of thousands of dollars worth of television equipment, and a lot of beer, in a Northern Albanian hovel, guarded by a Muslim, with a bottle of whisky, and an assault rifle. An Oxfam team showed up at the Adria and drank some of our beer. They were not aid workers but a PR/fundraising team, sent out to get pictures of the Oxfam aid workers, who had not yet arrived.

I tagged along with the principal NBC crew which was led by Fred Francis, a veteran war and Pentagon correspondent. His producer was Kevin Sites, a logistics magician, who had organised drivers, bodyguards and fixers, herded the techies and bribed the police. Fred boasted of the powerful American forces that would soon arrive, to kick Serbia's ass, although they didn't.[40] I stuck to Sites, who not only obviously knew what he was doing, but had seemingly unlimited supplies of cash.

So I went everywhere, up to the border where there was some

shooting and a train of miserable refugees crossing the border. It was one of those 'anyone here been raped and speak English' scenes. Although I eventually managed to interview a fleeing school teacher, who spoke French. I visited the OECD mission and interviewed a cynical Danish officer. I went to the hospital which stank and saw children with gunshot wounds. I saw everything but finally, after several days of Kukes, I had no idea who was winning the war, and only a vague notion of where it was happening. I could no longer tolerate the plumbing in the Bar Adria, so made my excuses and left, talking my way onto a French air force Puma helicopter for evacuation to the Mother Teresa International Airport in Tirana, 100km south.

I think I would have been a failure had I devoted myself to a career as a war correspondent. I know it's supposed to be glamorous but my heart wasn't in it. The plumbing in conflict zones is not the only reason. I completely lacked any of the detachment that I probably should have guarded.

That was a problem and also, there were far too many other reporters, almost all of them filing exactly the same made-up crap. There's an algorithm somewhere that says the greater the number of reporters present, the less likely that a useful story will emerge.

My gross ethical breach, if that's what it was, was when I became diverted from the journalism, to directly interfere in the progress of the conflict, albeit in no way that contributed to the eventual outcome.

It was the end of my second afternoon. Driving back to Kukes after a day in the mountains with the NBC crew, I saw a family on the side of the track, evidently terrified, miles from any reception point. I asked the driver to stop.

They were fleeing from across the border, in Kosovo, where Serbian troops and militias had attacked the neighbourhoods of ethnic Albanians. It was a religious and ethnic conflict. The Albanians spoke mostly the Albanian language Shqip and were mainly Muslims. The Serbs spoke Serbian and were Christians. It was a horrible mess. The Americans were now bombing the city and the family had fled through the mountains to the Albanian side of the frontier, where I found them. The girls were aged 8 and 10, their parents dressed respectfully but hardly for the mountains and the freezing nighttime temperatures. They had what they could carry, which wasn't much. Perhaps I intervened because they were so obviously a middle-class family, tugging at my class solidarity. He was wearing a tie, a desperate gesture, clinging on to a life that had been shattered. They were miles from anywhere. It pushed my buttons, anyway. I ordered my driver to stop and we took them on board.

On the drive to Kukes, I learned their story. The father, 40-something, was a dentist from Gjakova, or Đakovica as the Serbs called it. Large areas of the town had been completely destroyed. The Americans had bombed the Serbian police headquarters repeatedly, even though it was empty, but killing civilians in proximity. When I later visited Gjakova I saw this for myself. Scores of houses burned by the Serbs. An entire neighbourhood flattened by the Americans.

We drove down the mountain. The scenery of northern Albania is spectacular. Other than the periodic reports of distant mortars and crack of small arms, it might have been Switzerland. But there were no chalets or ski lifts. The landscape was marked only by the concrete bunkers that littered the entire country, built by the late paranoid Communist dictator Enver Hoxha.

It was a tight squeeze in the battered Mercedes station wagon. The Albanian driver shrugged his shoulders and didn't seem too worried. He was making more than he had seen in his life, thanks to the bottomless pockets of Kevin Sites. He kept his gun on his knees and the spare magazine in the place where normal people kept cassettes.

I took the family down to the U.N. refugee transit point by the new mosque. It stank and looked horrible but nobody was shooting at them. There was nothing else I could do. Taking them to the Adria wasn't an option. They would later be bussed down the terrifying road to Tirana, to a camp near the coast.

I subsequently wondered what had become of this family. So a year later, after the war subsided and most of the refugees had been repatriated, I travelled to Kosovo to see if I could find them. I bought gifts—some tea, some jam—at Gatwick Airport. And I did. I flew to Macedonia on a UN flight from Rome, then hired a driver to take me to Gjakova. There were Russian soldiers at the border. I bribed them with cans of Coke, to let me cross. I got to Djakova and asked around. It was a small town and it didn't take long to track them down. They were safe. The father had resumed his dental practice, amidst the uneasy peace of the Kumanovo agreement ending the war and demilitarising Kosovo. The children were in school. They wept when I arrived at their door, with my jam.

Journalism is betrayal, wrote Janet Malcolm in *The Journalist and the Murderer* (1989). 'Every journalist who is not too stupid or too full of himself to notice what is going on knows that what he does is morally indefensible.'

She has a point that journalists are fundamentally reptilian. I confess my motives were not solely humanitarian. I wanted to tell the story of this family, in every detail. I could see it as a cover for the *Sunday Times Magazine*.

So here I was, all poised for a gripping splash, but the family begged me not to. Even if I anonymised their names, they still feared retaliation. I could have written the story anyway. (Which I guess I just have, although I have waited 25 years.) But I promised silence.

It was at this moment that I realised I lacked the cold-blooded ruthlessness to be the reporter Malcolm describes. And I don't think I'm alone, after meeting hundreds or thousands of journalists in my time. We are not all terrible people.

But some are. There are journalists who are exactly like those Malcolm describes and I saw some of them in Albania. They feasted on misery. War correspondents might represent a brotherhood/sisterhood of sorts, but ultimately it wasn't a club I wanted to join. I was more comfortable where there was good plumbing, and fewer dilemmas.

Quite beyond my own very modest experience, there are big

problems with war reporting and the question that occurs to me is whether it's obsolete. Recent events around Israel and Ukraine suggest that for information on what's happening, hacks on the ground have been superseded by new technology. The best pictures are taken by drones and phone cameras, not by the television crews.

Do these powerful news gathering tools complement journalists, or make them redundant? Today, we hear much squealing from the usual suspects about the tight Israeli control on media access to Gaza, but what have we missed by the absence of Jeremy Bowen? Would letting in Western journalists really have made a difference to our understanding?

I have debated this point by email with Sarah Baxter, who was a brilliant section editor on the *Sunday Times* where she was a colleague, as was I, of the late Marie Colvin.[41]

Marie and I used to cadge Marlboro Lights from one another in the newsroom in Wapping, when she was in town. She was a gentle person, although tougher than I could ever be. Her usual habitats were the most dangerous places on earth. I occasionally handled her copy. She wasn't a great writer but was a fabulous reporter. After Marie was wounded and lost an eye in Sri Lanka, she returned to the fray, wearing an eyepatch, like a pirate. On 22 February, 2012, she was killed in Syria, in a targeted attack by the Assad regime, which loathed her. French prosecutors have launched a criminal prosecution against Assad regime officials believed responsible.

Marie was a wonderful brave journalist and there's no question she brought the horror of war to readers far away. Her attempts to shake Western countries to curb Assad were however entirely futile. Was Marie's death worth it?

Sarah, who is a very clever disruptive journalist of complicated Franco-American heritage, should have been editor of the *Sunday Times* but many are called and few are chosen. So she returned to Pennsylvania and now runs the Marie Colvin Center for International Reporting at Stony Brook University's School of Communication and Journalism, set up in her memory. It's run on a shoestring although Sarah has attracted a lot of support, including from News Corporation, although Sarah says please would I include a plea, should Rupert read this book, to please send more.

Sarah disagrees with me. 'War correspondents like Marie and Christina Lamb and others have been vital to exposing the kidnapping of Ukrainian children, Russian war crimes in Bucha and elsewhere, and the rapes of Israeli women on October 7. They are a voice for people who otherwise aren't heard.

'Marie did a great deal to establish this tradition. Christina has also written honestly about war fatigue among Ukrainian troops and civilians.

'If Western media were allowed into Gaza we would get just as many stories about Palestinian suffering but much more honest reporting about attitudes among civilians towards Hamas. At the moment, all the coverage is conducted on behalf of the Western media by Gazan journalists at great risk to themselves and their families, who are stuck there. Not only does this colour their reporting, they cannot report truthfully on Hamas because of fear of retribution.'

All good or fair points, except I am not convinced. I certainly have little faith in native Gaza journalists. Nobody reports independently from Gaza. The Gazan journalists supposedly at great risk are controlled by Hamas. The western journalists clamouring to get into Gaza would have been equally under the Hamas thumb.

Recent conflicts in Ukraine and the Middle East, with information provided by drones and geolocation and Open Source Intelligence, boosted by AI, is making the traditional war correspondent seem antiquated, like Boot in *Scoop*. At least, if your interest is knowing who is winning or losing any war, these technologies are much more illuminating than journalist boots on the ground. No matter how brilliant or bold, the vision of journalists is circumscribed if not manipulated.

I saw some horrible things in Kosovo and did a live satellite feed to viewers in America, saying what I'd seen. It made no difference, it was meaningless. This kind of journalism informs little and runs dangerously close to entertainment. It has become even more explicit thanks to social media platforms. It's easy now to watch soldiers dying and being mutilated. 'It's interesting when people die,' sang Don Henley in the movie Broadcast News. He had no idea.

Looking back at Kukes, I'm not sure any of us knew very much. I didn't. It was exactly like *Scoop*. We were chasing our own tails. The war correspondents prided themselves on proximity to the action but appeared unable to see the big picture, often magicked up the details, or resorted to cliches.

Others become partisans. I suppose they remind us that war is hell.

14

A SPY

In the land of the black lamb and grey falcon

I wasn't done with Albania. I was seduced by the country, like Rebecca West had been in her own masterpiece about the Balkans.[42] And like Tintin, my daemon and inspiration, I found the best stories where the other reporters were not. It's an inviolable Miller Rule of Journalism to stay away from the rat pack. In Tirana, with the help of my talented Albanian fixer, Gjergj, I tracked down Enver Hoxha's window Nexhmije in a tiny flat in a grimy suburb, a long way from her former billet downtown at the presidential palace. I found her editing a new edition of her husband's speeches, as if anyone wanted to read more of his wacko drivel. There was a fax machine she used to keep in touch with old comrades. There was quite a Hoxha diaspora, apparently. Some of them in London, working for the BBC's Albanian Service, I was told.

Nexhmije was elegantly dressed but had evidently lost weight after five years in prison for embezzlement, and we communicated via Gjergj in Italian. She was not especially gracious, this Lady Macbeth to a vicious dictator. She was lucky to escape hanging from a rope, considering what had happened to Elena Ceaușescu in Romania, executed after a kangaroo court trial in Bucharest with her husband Nicolae in 1989. My meeting with Nexhmije was a cracking story that didn't go anywhere at the time but would have been perfect for the *Spectator* Coffee House blog, had it existed at the time. *My coffee with Nexhmije*

92

would have been the headline. She died in 2020, aged 99.

Also in Tirana, I found an art therapy class in a refugee camp where displaced children were painting their experiences in the war zone and during their hair-raising evacuation. I had an early digital camera, recorded a dozen of the pictures, and filed from the internet café in Tirana, which was temporarily electrified. With the help of the local geeks, I got a very moving picture story off to MSNBC, who loved it.

Albania wasn't as poverty stricken as it looked. At the airport, I sat in on an American intelligence briefing warning that the country was infested with terrorists. I was later at a Kosovo Liberation Army training camp near the coast and they were pretty definitely terrorists, although temporarily on our side. But Albania was primarily a land of gangsters. (Many of them subsequently moved to Britain.) The collapse of the communist regime had left the criminals in charge of more or less everything.

I visited an enormous Kansas City-sized car lot outside Durrës, selling late-model European luxury cars with Swiss and German license plates. Stolen 'as is' or to special order. 'If there's anything you're looking for, let me know. I can get it for you in three days', I was assured by the Albanian proprietor, a Chinese TT pistol in his belt.

As a final fling in my mid-life Tintin odyssey I went down to the south of Albania for the *Sunday Times Magazine*, where a different tribe of mobsters had taken over. In Vlorë there were fleets of those Miami Vice-type cigarette boats that would go fast to Italy every night with drugs, guns and girls. If the smugglers were intercepted, they threw the girls in the water, to distract the Carabinieri.

With my two corrupt police bodyguards and my agile fixer Gjergj, we drove into the Pindus mountains to the compound of a gangster who offered to sell me a brick of heroin. He plonked it on the table in front of me, while offering me Suxhuk, an Albanian specialty featuring an unknown meat. I declined the Suxhuk from revulsion and the heroin in something resembling panic, mumbling something about how I would have to consult my principals in London. But it was a feeble riposte and I'm surprised he let me go, instead of feeding me to his pigs.

Gjergj had invented the impossible-to-believe cover story that I was a British intelligence officer. At least, I found it impossible to believe. Perhaps Albanians have different standards. This is a country, after all, where you shake your head to signify agreement. Also, in passing, to illustrate just what a weird country this was, Albania had a crush on Norman Wisdom. He was the only acceptable Western entertainer during Hoxha's rule. Hoxha apparently interpreted Wisdom's comic character as a metaphor for the downtrodden British proletariat's struggle against the bourgeoisie.

This ridiculous artifice that I was some kind of British agent was designed to explain my presence and perhaps keep me safe from anyone with doubts. Perhaps it was meant to be absurd. The gangster certainly didn't believe it. He presumably read it as a transparent cover story. I still don't know why he didn't shoot me. The guy had a sentry with a rocket-propelled grenade launcher. As was proving frequently the case in Albania, everyone in the room had guns but me. This was insanely dangerous but I was too much of an ingenue to realise it at the time.

We bid farewell to the gangster and drove on terrible roads to the deepest South of Albania, looking for cannabis plantations. We stopped at a settlement and spent the night in the house of the village chief. A great feast of dubious dishes was prepared for me, including sheep brain. Other than the guns—everyone as usual except me had an AK or a TT—it was a premodern scene. No television sets or satellite dishes. No cars, other than our (presumably stolen) FIAT minibus with Italian license plates. There was no electricity, not even an electrogen. The stars at night burn bright when it's this dark. It was hard to believe this was Europe. Yet the EU/Greek border was a few dozen kilometres away. I redeemed my inadequate appetite when I helped the village women call their sons on my satellite telephone. And it was strikingly the case that there were no young men present. They had all left to find their fortunes in Greece, Italy, Germany and England. I gave the chief $100 when I left, which to him was a fortune.

15

ANIMAL FARM

Surrey's Mean Fields—2001
'The truth is never pure and rarely simple'—Oscar Wilde

When the little war in Kosovo petered out, the world lost interest in
Albania, and the war reporters moved on. So did I. I had ticked the
war correspondent box. I was back in north London, with itchy feet.
Seized with the ill-advised fantasy of trading dinner at the Ivy with
lambing in the barn, a madness that seizes Londoners from time to
time, we traded our house in Hampstead for a 15th century farm-
house in Surrey, with everything imaginable wrong with it. The
escape to the country is a British cliché with its own TV show and
rarely works out well. Surrey has issues. Many of them are related to
the many awful snobby people who live there. But it was goodbye to
the Coffee Cup on Hampstead High Street, hello to the muck heap
next to the collapsing barn.

My life once again shadowed the Evelyn Waugh novel *Scoop*, in
which the hapless Boot is torn from his column, 'Lush Places'. After
paying a local youth to shovel the muck, I decided to try my hand as
an actual lush places correspondent, transmitting the vicissitudes of
the country to the metropolitans. Doubtless they could snortle at
the plastic peasant (me) trying to make hay. Self-deprecating humour
comes easily to me as there is much to deprecate.

But there was trouble ahead. Eleanor Mills, the editor of the
Sunday Times news review section, where this weekly paean was to be

published, and doubtless wound up by mischievous Witherow, said the gentle country life column I had imagined and proposed was instead to be called Mean Fields, in tribute to the Martin Scorsese film Mean Streets. We had heard enough of bucolic Britain, Mills said. She wanted grit and stink and encouraged me to be hard on my neighbours. A not-shabby sum was on offer for 750 words a week, which would pay for a lot of fodder, so rashly I agreed.

So there I was in the countryside with my horses, writing insults about my neighbours, who were it is true extremely boring and snobbish, and disparaging the Rector to boot. Adopting my most obnoxious air of entitlement, I chided him in my column for failing to call on me, since my recent installation as faux Lord of the Manor. Two days later he phoned and explained that he had just been in hospital for three weeks. Being a man of Christian charity, he subsequently invited me to the rectory for a cup of tea. He explained that he had found God in his previous career as a geologist. I subsequently discovered that many geologists have had odd epiphanies, hunting stones. I have since looked at them more carefully myself.

The 2001 foot-and-mouth cattle epidemic put an end to any further dreams of a quiet life. My plan to be a squire was consumed by another deep dive into the bottomless incompetence of British government and the cognate incompetence of the media.

Foot and mouth has faded from the collective memory but can be read as a preview of medical panics to come. I applied the Jim Dewey principle of questioning the accepted narrative and taking charge of the investigation myself. It was so obvious that everything the government was doing was irrational that I questioned whether I was missing something. But the harder I looked, the more insane the policy. The media herd, dumber than cattle, was swallowing the government's lines and lies and was posing no serious questions.

As later with Covid, the pack of star political correspondents took charge of the coverage and the story turned into Westminster theatre full of sound and fury and remote from any scientific understanding or appreciation of what was occurring in the countryside.

Why? The media is stuffed with graduates who read history, politics and economics and have no scientific aptitude at all. Political correspondents are the worst. Many have attended Oxford University, a finishing school of arrogance and imbecility. They demonstrated no comprehension or competence.

Replete with horrors, lies and scandal, Foot and Mouth was a very good story. It was in truth a political and economic illness, not even a serious disease, manipulated by malevolent players for cash. It was the equivalent for most cattle of a cold and never the horrific plague promoted by the media. Many of my colleagues are susceptible to hysteria when writing about scientific subjects they don't understand, as we were to see later when the elite political correspondents completely succumbed to hypomania during Covid.

Elemental to understanding foot and mouth is the problem that it is more or less impossible to tell if an animal is sick just by looking at it. The government got around this by slaughtering animals even when they were healthy. Slaughtering healthy animals on suspicion they had been exposed was wildly disproportionate and the beef barons collected windfall compensation. It's still unclear how many healthy animals were killed, often in brutal conditions. Perhaps 10 million.

I reported in the *Sunday Times* that there was an effective inoculation to protect cattle against foot and mouth but its use had been banned by the Ministry of Agriculture because the EU would accept only unvaccinated meat. So that was the smoking gun. The sickness was the regulation. Not that exports of British beef to the EU were significant. I talked to a senior vet in Israel and asked what they did about foot and mouth there. They let the animals get better and treat secondary infections with antibiotics, he told me. They use vaccines as a cordon sanitaire around infections, not slaughter. I discovered that there is no human hazard from eating beef that had been vaccinated.

The powerful ruling members of the National Farmers Union collected £1 billion in compensation for slaughtered animals. But small farmers were devastated. Healthy rare breed sheep were exterminated and pet goats were slaughtered. 'Stamp it out,' was the cry from the NFU. Which was obediently done by the government. Even the legality of the cull was questionable, although nobody was held accountable. Vets broke their oaths to protect animals by colluding in the slaughter of animals that were not sick.

The government's senior scientific adviser in this affair, predictably, was Professor Neil Ferguson of Imperial College London. His models were hysterical.[43] But using a playbook that has subsequently become familiar, anyone dissenting from the policy of slaughtering healthy animals was branded a crank and animal-rights activist. The charge didn't land on me. I was hardly an animal rights fanatic. I'd been hunting with the Old Surrey and Burstow. I'd driven my own sheep to the slaughter house

I was merely asking questions. What was disheartening but not surprising was that almost all the other journalists were not. They were repeating government and NFU lies and talking points and demanding that more animals be killed faster.

The agriculture minister at the time was one Nick Brown. He went on to have a long political career, eventually abruptly terminated in murky circumstances. He was useless and gutless. His ministry was the most indolent in Whitehall, spending its time kowtowing to the NFU and doling out subsidies to the barley barons. After I organised a demonstration of outraged *Sunday Times* readers outside, protesting the devastation in the countryside, Brown finally invited me to his office at the Ministry. He wasn't interested in answering my questions and instead weirdly talked about the music scene in Newcastle. Was he flirting? Recollecting The Animals, whom he said were boyhood friends, he even sang a few bars to me from The House of the Rising Sun. Which I taped. We ridiculed him in the *Sunday Times*. None of it mattered. Brown was an MP, minister, whip and opposition front bencher for four decades before he was forced in 2022 to leave Keir Starmer's opposition team in circumstances that Starmer refuses to explain.

Eventually the then prime minister, Tony Blair, declared he had taken personal command of the foot and mouth crisis, and made it worse by accelerating the entirely unnecessary slaughter, with the unwilling help of the Army. Blair subsequently passed the 2004 Civil Contingencies Act to remove any doubt of the government's authority during a future emergency, including ordering the slaughter of healthy animals.

I was congratulated for great work by the Editor but the truth is that nobody in charge took any notice. Magnus Linklater, one of Britain's most solid journalists, smelt a rat, too. Otherwise I was a lonely voice. It was one of those scandals that in Britain seems quickly forgotten. My efforts to subvert the government's policy were a complete failure.

Abigail Woods,[44] the distinguished professor of veterinary history, subsequently wrote the definitive book exposing this entire racket. She was also ignored. When foot and mouth broke out again in 2007 as a result of a lab leak at the government's own animal health laboratory at Pirbright in Surrey, they started slaughtering all over again. I was the first journalist to draw the link between the proximity of the lab and the outbreak of foot and mouth downstream. The other journalists were too thick to notice.

16

EXILE

France—2001

'Into the face of the young man who sat on the terrace of the Hotel Magnifique at Cannes there had crept a look of furtive shame, the shifty hangdog look which announces that an Englishman is about to speak French'—P.G. Wodehouse

My heart really wasn't in the English countryside and honestly the countryside wasn't that into me. My family might have been peasants four or five generations back. I had learned to drive the school tractor at Bedales, but only to take it out joyriding on the local roads. I was not just ill-suited for farming, but had become rather widely unloved. I had annoyed many of my neighbours in my column, as required by Eleanor Mills. But, the truth is, I didn't really want to fit in anyway.

I was distracted by my own midlife crisis/need for a change of scenery/something completely different, which ultimately I resolved by moving to France where I wrote a book on 21st-century France[45] inspired by the *Devil's Dictionary* authored by the troublemaking American newspaperman Ambrose Bierce. Published as *France, A Nation on the Verge of a Nervous Breakdown* it led to me becoming a dissident commentator on French politics and culture.

Rupert Wright, a colleague at the doomed *European*, had just bought a house near Pézenas and I came down to look around. Rupert was a clever, versatile journalist, a bit of a rogue like me, and was writing a book about the Languedoc, so was full of local knowledge. We drove around looking at ancient relics and as we passed through the village that was to become mine. Rupert pointed at an imposing although somewhat dilapidated Maison de Maître and said it was for sale. We parked, rang the doorbell, met the owner, looked around and I bought it then and there on a handshake, being temporarily long on inherited cash, which otherwise I would have squandered on something stupid like a Porsche. It was the price of a studio apartment in Camden. I called Mrs Miller to announce that we were now the owners of a starter chateau and fortunately she was forgiving. I had whimsically purchased more than a house but an entirely new life, opening new chapters for my journalism and much else.

I have always had a little France in my heart, maybe because of *Tintin*, although he was Belgian. But I knew little about the village or the region or even, as it turned out, a great deal about France when I made my purchase. All have turned out to be far more complicated than I had imagined. The village was at least 1000 years old, built in a pattern called a *'circulade'* around the church, with narrow and charming little streets, *ruelles*, in concentric rings. Traces of the ancient ramparts were in place. They had been built to defend against marauding Visigoths.

My new home was in the heart of the ancient royal province of Languedoc, now included within the super-region of Occitanie, stretching from the Mediterranean and the mouth of the Rhône river to Toulouse, the Pyrenees and Spanish border. It was a reorganisation engineered to dilute the strength of the populist National Front by socialist President François Hollande. Languedoc is so-called because of its Occitan language in which the word for yes is *'oc'* not *'oui'* as in French. Few now speak it. But what intrigued me was that it was the centre of Catharism, a dualistic religious faith regarded as heretical by the Vatican. The Cathars believed the Earth was the work of the devil. The crucifixion was an illusion, the physical body meaningless. The pope launched a brutal crusade in the 13th century to eliminate the Cathars,[46] and mostly succeeded. Still, there are surviving heretics. Including, now, me.

Everyone has been here, Celts, Phoenicians, Greeks and Romans. And now of course exiles from northern Europe, for whom Occitanie has become a sort of French Florida. The Romans built the Via Dometia, original parts of which can still be discovered, other parts were destroyed for the A9 autoroute: the corridor is a river of commerce, then and now. The contrast with affluent, snooty Surrey was striking. There were no cows, there were vines. There was no grassy Downsland, but craggy garrigue. The village where I had impulsively implanted myself was neither wealthy nor pretentious. There was a bar, a butcher and three boulangeries.

I kept a foot in both England and France for a while. The house in France was but a *maison secondaire* but from 2010, Mrs M was spending more and more time in London on the Olympic project. So I spent more and more time in France. Then, a blow. As I was moving to and fro, I'd attempted to subvert the Mean Fields brief with dispatches from France as occasional leavening but as I spent more and more time in France and less and less in the Mean Fields, the editor John Witherow wasn't wearing it. He abruptly gave my column to Jeremy Clarkson, the star of Top Gear, who was his Notting Hill neighbour and celebrated car bore. Clarkson later went farming himself, but monetised it, via Amazon Prime.

I met Clarkson just once at Witherow's very grand house in Notting Hill. He was extremely annoyed with me for a column I had just written disparaging the idea that Top Gear represented public broadcasting. He was offended and said the show made a fortune for the BBC, which wasn't really the point. That his show went on to find commercial success on Amazon Prime is QED as far as I'm concerned. Nevertheless, I wish him well in his farming venture. I've been there and done that. Suitable footwear and a supplemental income are the keys. I note he has bought a Lamborghini tractor. I would have recommended John Deere.

The depths of a 1000-year-old French village cannot be discovered on a two-week holiday. It's been a journey of 25 years so far. It didn't help that my language skills were basic at first. It was only when a neighbour showed up on my doorstep one evening and presented me with a stray dog that I started to cut through. Walking a dog is a vector to acceptance everywhere and with Ringo at my side, I was soon making friends with all the other dog owners in the village.

Surprisingly the mayor was not a peasant, a *plouc*,[47] but a professor and head of pharmaceutical research at the University of Montpellier, a village boy made good at a time when French national education could reliably put bright kids on a social escalator. He was pleased to have what he imagined to be a distinguished British journalist as a resident and held a drinks party (a *'cocktail'*) to introduce me to the village notables.

He was also of course a politician and thought it might add some interest to his electoral list at the forthcoming elections to decorate it with an Englishman, eligible in those pre-Brexit days to serve as an elected local representative in France. He asked, I accepted. I made a clumsy speech when we held a pre-election rally at the Salle du Peuple. And then I was swept into power, along with everyone else on the list. It was hardly a personal political triumph.

It is said that all political careers end in failure but mine began that way when I realised the mayor had no interest in my grand designs and would run things as he always had with his first deputy and the head of technical services. I did persuade him to install an electric car recharge point in front of the sports hall. That was the summit of my political career.

I lost my eligibility to serve on the council after Brexit, although subsequently regained it by obtaining an Irish passport (thanks to grandma Edith) and could have run again. But I'd served my time. I learned lots about France and did improve my French. But my political career is done, other than as an ill-tempered commentator. And even if France seems to be in perpetual chaos, my verdict on local government in France, from someone who saw it close up, is that it's pretty good, compared to the British version. The bins get emptied three times a week, there are no potholes and when there was a burglary Marc the municipal policeman caught the perp.

The immediate challenge was the language. It's one thing to order a coffee at a cafe, quite another to make a speech at the municipal council. The inadequacy of my French was quickly evident and accompanied by Ringo, I repaired the deficiencies by joining the morning coffee klatch of village elders, listening, essaying the occasional joke.

Shopkeepers bore the brunt of my errors. Clumsy interaction is how I learned that a *baguette* is feminine and a tyre is not a penoo. Learning French is like serving time in a Soviet Gulag, or so I suppose, because I never have. The first 10 years are probably the hardest. And then suddenly, one day, it clicks. You're speaking French. Subjunctives and all. It is never possible to extinguish the English accent but that's not a problem because weirdly the French find an English person speaking French to be charming. But pronunciation is very important or your *oeuf à la coque* might turn into a Coke.

Charles V supposedly spoke Italian to women, French to men, German to his horse, and Spanish to God. I discovered that as my French got better, I forgot how to say things in English. My dog appears to be bilingual.

My struggle to master French turned out not just to have practical implications but made me think about language more deeply and why journalists must not be monoglot. To have a second language is to have another soul. As I learned to speak French, first like a 'vache espagnole,' a Spanish cow, as francophones describe those struggling with the language of Molière, and then comfortably, I learned much more about my mother tongue, became a much better journalist, and I am certain my writing in English is better.

If I was the God of journalism, I would demand that mastery of a foreign language be obligatory. It's essential because it unlocks an entirely new dimension in the brain. It's true that as an Anglophone one can 'get by' almost anywhere. It's not the same as fluency in another language and the door it opens to new ways of thinking and writing. Edward Luttwak, a smart writer on security, thinks a lot of western intelligence failures are because the spies are monoglot. So are most journalists.

17

SURELY NOT THE ROYALS

Except this—2014

I have always avoided writing about celebrities although I know that celebs used to sell newspapers and now score very highly in the metrics measuring reader engagement. I know little about them and confuse Kardashian with Britney Spears. At the top of the celebrity pecking order are royals and while I have never made them my beat, have run into some from time to time. I would normally avoid as too ghastly the biggest royal story of this century, the Shakespearean tragedy of Prince Harry and Meghan Markle. But I did get a look at this and so I will share what I saw.

In circumstances that discretion obliges me to obscure, I had dinner with Prince Harry at Buckingham Palace after the first London Invictus Games in 2014. Or to be strictly honest, I was the Plus One of somebody more important.

The food was excellent, the state dining room impressive although in general the palace looked a little tired, and in need of more than a lick of paint. Harry was charming, fluently delivering an after-dinner speech, conscientiously thanking his collaborators. Although I wasn't paying especially close attention, since the attractive and very drunk daughter of a senior politician was flirting with me throughout, under the influence of Her Late Majesty's cellar. The unkind would say that a woman might well have had to have had a drink or two, to pay any attention to me. But the wine was very good.

I was also a guest at the opening ceremony of the first Invictus Games at the Olympic Park in east London, and saw a happy Harry with his proud father and brother, genuine delight on their faces as the wounded soldiers, some in wheelchairs, paraded before them. I was practicing my French with a couple of generals from the French army, which was represented at the event by a number of wounded soldiers.

The picture on the front page of *The Times* the next day told the story of a father and his sons at peace with themselves. There was no inkling of the horrors and fiascos to follow: Oprah, Spotify, Netflix, American Riviera Orchard.

Later I was in Toronto at the second games, and was an eyewitness to Harry's blossoming romance with Meghan. They sat together in Nathan Phillips Square to watch wheelchair basketball, and it was already obvious that nobody could take their eyes off the couple. That evening, I sat near Ivana Trump in the Scotiabank Arena when Harry took to the stage, welcoming and thanking the athletes.

This was before Harry succumbed fully to early onset midlife crisis. That seemed to happen later, after the wedding the following year, when the first red flags appeared. In Canada, in 2017, he still had a blessed touch to him, like his mother. I had spent an evening with her shortly before she was killed in 1997, at a *Sunday Times* party at the Banqueting House, and her effect was mesmerising. After being presented to her, Peter Millar, one of the most hardened journalists I've ever known, held out his hand and said to me, 'I'm not washing this until I've gone home and used it.'

Harry had had a decent turn in the army. He was liked by his men. Fellow officers (including my former son in law) respected him. I was never clear why he felt he should leave the Army when he did. His need for protection probably made him more trouble than he was worth. So he was a second son who needed a job. In the Ottoman and Mughul empires, such problems were solved by fratricide. But with Invictus, it seemed to me, he had found a befitting role, as a liaison between the Armed Forces and the Royal Family.

Sometimes you get the best observations in the smoker's sinbin. In Toronto, I was catching a fag outside the headquarters Sheraton hotel, next to the wheelie bins, with some American women, the wives of the wounded Americans participating in the games. That morning, Prince Harry had visited the American camp set up in one of the hotel banqueting rooms.

One of the women told me a story. She was standing watching the prince make his way through the room shaking hands. She called out to him, asking if she could take a selfie with him. Shaking his head, a protection officer interposed himself and said no.

And then, a little cameo of his empathy. Harry overruled his bodyguard, turned to the woman and said, 'But of course you can.' And then followed perhaps a highlight of this woman's life. Her husband had been wounded in Iraq. She had suffered, too. But now this! Her selfie, the handsome prince's arm around her shoulders, had already been posted on the Facebook page of her church in Georgia. This was soft diplomacy par excellence.

Invictus continues but the wars in Iraq and Afghanistan are over and the games have lost their purity of purpose. The eligibility has been stretched to include servicemen who have hurt themselves in motorcycle accidents. But it's no longer about wounded warriors. The Invictus games have become a spectacle featuring Harry and Meghan. Harry has been lost as an advocate for the Armed Forces, exiled in the gilded prison of Montecito, desperately unhappy, immersed in litigation, terrified of the media, pressured by Netflix to be something he isn't. Meghan is desperate, too. She kissed a prince, who turned into a frog.

It takes living in a republic, as I do, to appreciate the usefulness of the monarchy, however absurd. But there's a price being paid by those within it.

There's something going on here that's more than fodder for the papers. We are in some kind of trance, hypnotised by this human tragedy. The Sussex story is poisonous, like all celebrity journalism. It plays to a cruel voyeurism. The subjects of this, whether they be royals or television presenters, become objects, and many are driven mad by it. It's the media as a snake, eating its own tail. There's a cruelty to our voyeurism but we shall never be sated. At least my colleagues on the royal beat might indulge our obsession with a sense of shame.

18

HOMAGE TO CATALONIA

The Ghost of a Lost Cousin
'In Spain, the dead are more alive than the dead of any other country in the
world'—Federico Garcia Lorca

In my corner of France, the Pyrenees are not far away. On dog patrol, I can see the Pic de Canigou, the sacred mountain of Catalonia, looming on the southwest horizon, covered in snow. I am in France with a foot in Spain. My village is stuffed with people named Lopez, Martinez and Sanchez. Some of the elders speak Catalan. Many families came here as refugees after the Spanish Civil War.

I'd been interested for years in the story of my second cousin, Morris Miller, a Jewish communist from Hull killed fighting for the Republic in the Spanish Civil War. He was 22. Because I was curious, I decided to be a war correspondent once again, this time of a battle that occurred 70 years ago.

Morris was a mythic figure in my family but nobody knew much about what had happened to him, after he vanished from Hull in the aftermath of the violent clashes of local communists with Oswald Mosely's black shirts at the battle of Corporation Field in Hull in 1936. Morris customarily ate Sunday lunch at his uncle's house but annoyed everyone with his rants. He'd stalked out after an outburst accusing his affluent uncle of being a 'dirty capitalist' and hadn't been seen again.

But his destination was obvious. Before his flit, he had spoken to his cousins of the Spanish Civil War as the epochal struggle, the essential confrontation with the dark forces of fascism and Nazism menacing Jews and the world. This was delusional in the light of subsequent events because it wasn't an epochal struggle but merely a sideshow but at the time it was the shibboleth of the anti-fascist left and the Communist Party of Great Britain, of which Morris was a passionate member.

It was technically a crime under the British non-intervention law to openly join the Spanish Republicans but there was a well-worn route nevertheless, entering France as a 'tourist'. France was strongly sympathetic to the Spanish Republicans.[48] The communist railway workers (*cheminots*) smuggled the volunteers to Perpignan on the southern border, where they crossed the Pyrenees into Spain.

I knew that Morris was killed in August 1938, in a battle outside Gandesa, in what turned out to be the final doomed offensive of the Republicans. They were defeated on the battlefield and betrayed by Stalin, who stole their gold and sent them junk weapons. The secret Molotov-Ribbentrop pact[49] between Germany and the Soviet Union was signed days after Morris was killed. Stalin abandoned the Spanish republicans to their fate. Morris's death hadn't retarded the advance of fascism in Europe by two minutes.

So was it noble? Principled? Foolish? Misguided? Naive? Some combination of all of the above. Mainly, not much was known.

My quest began with a blank slate and took three years to complete. There were intriguing questions but there was not much to go on. Morris' mother had destroyed his papers as World War Two began, fearful the Nazis were about to invade and they would incriminate the family as communists. So that was a blow. But I found out lots, nonetheless, about what happened after he left Hull, which is where the story builds to its grim conclusion.

I visited Spain four times retracing Morris's story, including riding a horse over the Pyrenees to recreate his journey from France to Spain. Perhaps a little fanciful as I didn't know the route. But suggestive of what these guys endured, just to join the fight.

The New York University Tamiment Library,[50] with its extensive archives were a treasure trove. Here I found articles Morris had written for the *Volunteer for Liberty* newspaper. He was a fine writer, ideologically obsessed but with an eye for detail.

The Spanish Civil War is and was a tremendous story and everyone from Hemingway to Orwell was there.[51] Books and films continue to appear. The volunteer International Brigade which Morris joined is embedded in Communist mythology but the real story is that it was ineptly led, barely equipped, ill-trained and ultimately betrayed and defeated. This is not the preferred narrative.

After arriving in Spain, Morris Miller would have been processed through the training camp at Tarazona, near Albacetes and have been ready for action by early 1938. After very basic training, he was badly wounded almost as soon as he arrived on the battlefield in Caspe, between Zaragoza and Tarragona. He was stalked around a tree and fired at five times at close range and left for dead. An ambulance had picked him up.

That summer, he returned to battle in the forefront of the fighting on the southwest side of the great Ebre (Ebro) river southwest of Barcelona. This was supposed to be a game-changing offensive in which the Republican army would cross the river on pontoons, and attack Franco's Nationalists, disrupting their advance on Barcelona and perhaps turning the course of the war.

In fact, the mission was hopeless from the start, as an ill-equipped army lacking logistics and air cover was thrown forward to be chewed to pieces by the Nationalists, with superior arms, professional formations and competent leadership. The amateur army of the Republicans (the Communists to all intents and purposes by this stage) was duly slaughtered. Morris Miller did not survive this fight and neither did the International Brigade which was disbanded soon after and its members repatriated. It was seen off from Barcelona with the promise from the mythical Communist firebrand La Pasionaria[52] that they would not be forgotten. She was also famous for proclaiming *¡no pasarán!* (the enemy shall not pass) which of course they did.

Miller's greatest legacy was in fact as a journalist, although he was also a bold soldier. He left a vivid account of the military disaster, even if you are forced to read between the lines. There's a verisimilitude to the stories written by soldiers that is often lacking in the formulaic coverage of war correspondents.

As the battle started, the communist leaders at first persuaded themselves that they had got off to a good start. Franco, a far shrewder general, with trained Moroccan mercenaries and German aircraft, had allowed the Republicans to cross the river while preparing his own revenge. The Republicans assembled in great camps and played football with the locals. Then they advanced on the Nationalists in a manoeuvre that ranks in the annals of military incompetence with the charge of the Light Brigade at Balaclava. Their soldiers lacking even water at times, the Republicans were cut to pieces by German-supplied artillery and aircraft, directed by Franco himself from a nearby mountain top.

Miller's account of this battle is highly revealing of a disastrous strategic and tactical situation, albeit the Communists could not directly admit it. His articles include absurdly propagandistic spin— 'for we licked them as surely as though we had taken additional terrain. They hoped to blow us off that hill by sheer weight of flying steel. Well they hammered us but it was not hard enough.'

But the Republican military disaster is forcefully there, too. On Hill 481 (its height in metres), the Republican commanders threw their barely-equipped soldiers into an un-winnable position. Forced off the mountain, the Republicans repeated their mistake. They fought next from the even more impossible position on notorious Hill 666. When I stopped at the Guardia Civil post in Gandesa to get directions, the Cabo knew exactly what I was looking for. '*La colina del diablo*,' he said—the hill of the devil.

Hill 666 today is heavily wooded and alongside the modern road from Gandesa to the coast. There is a small, unmarked turn-off where you can climb the mountain, penetrating out of earshot of the passing heavy trucks, laden with the commerce of the region's huge market gardens and orchards.

The slope is scarred by ancient shell splinters. Much land has slipped from ancient terraces, now overgrown. The idea of Morris's commanders was to get behind the ridge of the hill, but once there, there was little they could do except absorb punishment. They didn't have the airpower or artillery to counter the Nationalists. Somehow they had persuaded themselves that this was how they would win the war.

There was nothing glamorous about the death of Morris. One of 526 British volunteers who did not return from Spain, he was one minute there, one minute gone, cut down by a shell fragment on the lee side of the hill. The flinty rock of the hill made it an ideal place to drop bombs and shells with great effect. It is impossible to dig proper trenches or fortifications, though there are visible scrapes into the hillside that might have afforded a little shelter. Anyone in the open was asking for trouble. The great natural frontier of Catalonia was where the Communists sacrificed their bravest and most militant young soldiers, for nothing.

Alan Warren, a Spanish civil war researcher who lives in Barcelona shared the most astonishing material of all, an unpublished memoir of the Welsh miner Billy Griffiths, a communist militant and union activist who was himself among the more striking figures in the international brigade and a fine writer.

The Griffiths memoir unlocked the story of Morris's death and is also in itself an beautifully written testament. I had not just discovered Morris, but this extraordinary Welsh miner, a working class communist, and an incredible writer with a great story to tell. His diary includes unique, dramatic and important recollections of Morris during the battle on the Ebro. And it takes the story to the final very abrupt killing of Miller by shellfire.

Griffiths takes up the story before the great battles in the Sierra Pandols, and his manuscript, almost filmic, with a soldier's eye for terrain and place, describes an army poorly provisioned, although the commissars at headquarters made sure they were fed. I share his story because nobody else has.

'Our food was quite monotonous. It hardly varied-bread and coffee for breakfast; buns for dinner and lentils for supper. However there was some slight advantage in being attached to HQ. After dinner, and sometimes after supper, Monty Sim's batman brought out the scraps for disposal into an improvised bin. All eyes were fixed on him as he scraped the plates clean and when he had gone, there was a concerted rush to delve among the scraps.

'It was an undignified sight. These were cultured men. Hickman, the head of the observers, had led a sheltered life. Prep school, Public school, Cambridge, a degree and an apprenticeship with Dunlop, then Spain. Joe Latus, a trawler captain; an American news reporter and so on. Yet the scraps were irresistible: a bit of liver or meat on a bone, perhaps a potato. It was a change.'

On the advance to Corbera on July 25/26th, Griffiths picked two men to scout the road towards Corbera. He chose Morris and 'a fellow from Swansea'. He noted that Morris though young was already a seasoned campaigner. The Swansea fellow was very young, and it was his 'first experience'.

'We moved leisurely through trees laden with fruit-black luscious figs, pomegranates, grapes. It was like the garden of Eden! We climbed upwards until we arrived at a prominence overlooking Corbera. There was nothing to report. There seemed little movement. On the way back we took the shortest direction to the road, calculating that the battalion would have moved forward to that point.'

'Suddenly we came across a camp! There were horses and men. Morris and I assumed them to be Moorish cavalry. Our companion became hysterical and wanted to run down and join them, insisting they were our men. This could not be. We had no cavalry! We pulled him down and Miller sat on his head until he regained his composure. We told him to take the long way back to keep out of danger. This he did. In the meantime, Miller and I crept closer to the camp. We came across a mule loaded with rifles and immediately decided to pinch it. Scarcely daring to breathe we untied the animal and led it away.

'When we reached the road at a point a few miles further down, we found ourselves under fire. We scampered off the road and lay behind a bank. To our right was a house. I hung onto the mule while Miller went to investigate. It was a temporary Brigade Headquarters. The British Battalion were in action, attacking some strongpoint in the hills on the other side of the road. We left the mule in the care of the officer in charge, telling him he could have the rifles, but the animal was ours. Having done this we dashed across the road to join the Battalion.

'We were ordered to enter Corbera and look for grub. We set off, three of us on the back of the mule. The place was deserted. They had left in a hurry. There were masses of stores. Tinned milk, tinned food of all kinds and lots and lots of boots. We drank a few tins of milk, and while Dobson searched for a pair of boots to fit him, Miller and I went to look for a cart. We found one, and a harness. Soon the mule was hitched up, the cart loaded and we were on our way.'

After being driven off Hill 481, a disaster by Morris's own account, the British battalion went into reserve, returning to the front on the evening of August 15th, to the deadly Hill 666.

'It was good to relax. Hot coffee in the morning and evening. Even the carrabunces and lentils seemed more appetizing. I had a parcel from home-the only one I ever received! Cigarettes from the local club, salmon, chocolate. This was indeed luxurious living! Morris Miller and I were making a dugout. Most people thought us daft, but I was always over cautious. We had stopped work to share out the parcel. I didn't smoke, so the cigs were a free distribution. A fair crowd had gathered and we sat around eating chocs and generally gossiping. Half a dozen planes came over and dropped a few bombs. The crowd melted like magic. All went into the dugout, piled on top of each other.

All that is, except me and Miller. We were the only two left outside. There was no room for any more. It was quite a joke. At least, they thought so!'

'August 15th'

'That evening I shared blankets with Lesser. The food truck came at dawn, and Lesser had gone down to the road to wait for it. The road continued in the direction of our rear in a straight line for about half a mile along a narrow valley, no more than 20 yards wide flanked by steep hills. To the right of where I sat, the terrain took on a new and more sinister appearance. It was as if a giant's hand had cut a cleft through the mountain, revealing the rocks in all its nakedness below.'

'Through the jungle of boulders and projecting needle-like rocks, dwarfing a man by their size, a narrow tortuous path wound its way from the road, skirting precipitous drops where cleavage was sharpest and running onto the open at a point to the right, on the rising hills behind our position. Skirting the head of the ravine, the path got lost in a more open stretch of level ground, before the hills rose again, sharply to the crest and the front line positions of the British Battalion. One tried to avoid as much as possible the path and open ground because of the intensity of shell and mortar fire, which at times, came over at the rate of 40 per minute. Yet this was the only way to the British battalion HQ, the Canadian positions and the front line.

'I got caught twice, but each time was fortunate to be near a shallow slit trench. Morris was not so lucky. He was killed outright!! So also was the Chief of Fortifications for the Brigade (Egan Schmidt), who with his staff, was caught in a barrage not far from the Brigade HQ. He and three of his staff were killed and a number wounded.'

I climbed to the spot where Morris Miller died and looking at the concrete marker with his name. I wished I could have felt other than that his death had been completely in vain. At least, starting from zero, I'd done justice to his story. The lessons of the Morris

Miller story are many. First, that there's always more to be discovered. Next, that the conventional narrative of the Spanish Civil War does not survive contact with the actuality. If it was a heroic struggle against fascism it was also a complete mess. Then, there's reaffirmation of my theory that the best stories are to be found away from the press pack. Be like the cat. Walk alone. Lastly, it's a testament to the value of slow journalism. It was curiosity that propelled me. Curiosity is the key virtue of a journalist. It's the difference between stenography and investigation.

I have taught a few courses at the *Haute École de Journalisme* in Montpellier and the most depressing element of the job was the absence of this fundamental curiosity of too many of my students. There's a timidity and fragility, too. I have heard this complaint from others who teach. I fear that without curiosity no journalist is ever going to go far. It's one thing to ask ChatGPT about the battle of the Ebro. Quite another to climb a mountain littered with shell fragments to discover a rough concrete marker with the name of a relative who was killed there, eighty years earlier.

It's curiosity that creates the serendipity of discovery. When I was researching this story, initially about just Morris, I also discovered Griffiths, and in the library in New York, a letter from an American soldier, not Morris but one of his comrades, to his sweetheart. In the envelope I found a dried flower that he'd sent her from Spain. It was an extraordinary moment. So, this was my best story, and the one that took longest.

19

RESCUED BY MACRON

I Bawl at the Gaul—2015

The French are frequently caricatured by British journalists, mocked for a lengthy list of supposed defects including even, *pace* Kelvin MacKenzie, dodgy food. It is true that they eat at McDonald's a million times a day, the national dish is pizza, which is sometimes sold in vending machines and that they often make it with the wrong kind of cheese, Emmental not Mozzarella. There is even a journalistic sub-genre for this. It's called froggie bashing. I have frequently been accused of such bashing and angrily plead not guilty. I adore France and the French. When I am rude to them, it is because I love them. Also, unlike my experience in Surrey, few people in my village can read my articles, so I'm not widely hated here.

Without my column, I wrote a book, mostly to prove I could. It wasn't exactly froggie-bashing, though some misread it as this. The exercise was as much for me to discover France for myself as as for readers to learn about the France I uncovered. You can't understand the big picture, without first getting to grips with the details. And I discovered plenty. I uncovered some fascinating stories, as well as a lot about French political, economic and social failings.

The best of the stories I uncovered was told to me by the village doyen, Jean-Louis Souquet, who was 14 on the day of liberation in 1944. During the occupation, there had been a gun battle on the plateau that rises behind the village, after a British Sterling bomber from Tunisia had dropped containers containing explosives, guns and gold Louis Napoleon coins to the local resistance, the Maquis Bir-Hakeim.

The plan was to equip the *maquis* (resistance) to stir up trouble, diverting attention from the forthcoming invasion of Normandy. But the drop had been observed by German sentries in the church tower and they scrambled the troops (who were billeted in what was later my house), and there was a gun battle in which 17 German soldiers were killed and 22 wounded.

In the midst of this, three village boys succeeded in stealing the container with the money. The German commander in Béziers was furious and ordered the village levelled.[53] The village was only saved from bombardment because the senior German officer here, a superannuated Prussian who wore a monocle, was shacked up with a local girl. He persuaded his senior officer to spare the village, peddling the unlikely claim that the villagers hadn't known anything about it. The money was never recovered and even now it is a sensitive subject.

Another grand adventure was my visit to the tomb of the exiled Napoleon III at an abbey in Hampshire, in my quest to understand the Second Empire. It is guarded by Benedictine monks fiercely protecting the Emperor from the efforts of the French government who want him back, or what remains of him. I was escorted to the Emperor's presence by the Abbot. Napoleon rests in a mausoleum in an imposing sarcophagus donated by Queen Victoria, who wrote fondly of him in her diaries.

Where I do bash the French it is mainly on the point of what I have come to believe has been their grossest geopolitical miscalculation. The French elite is consumed with suspicion of Britain and America while obsessed with cosying up to the Germans. Anglophobia is embedded in France for obvious reasons, given the history, even after the Entente Cordiale and Britain rescuing France twice from the '*boches*' (Germans). After the war, this hatred of the Anglo Saxons was baked in by the hyper-Anglophobic General De Gaulle. He hated the British despite or perhaps because we saved his bacon. But the British ought to be the best friends of France, not the Germans, I argued.

The huge mistake aligning themselves with the Germans, not the British, after the war, was compounded by clinging to the leder-hosen after the unification of Germany. That diluted French influence and expanded German power. Subsequently, in every recent dispute in the EU, the Germans have proven to be in charge. The French would have done better embracing the '*rosbifs*' (us). Together we would have been a formidable counterweight to the Germans. Britain and France would have been stronger together, was my view, doubtless coloured by being British in France.

The refusal of the French to follow my wise advice has been a catastrophic, historic sequence of events. Refusal to reset when the Wall came down was the cause of Brexit and much else, in my amateur opinion. And now look at the mess. The country is broken. Nearly half the population fears civil war. But from chaos comes wonderful stories. All but two of us in the morning coffee klatch have died now, including Jean-Louis, the last witness to the occupation. I miss him and his stories.

20

THE NAKED EMPEROR

Jupiter aligns with Mars—2017

After writing the book, I found myself spending far too much time doing not very much at all. It was Andrew Neil who prodded me from my lethargy. Andrew lives on the posh Provençal side of the Rhône while we're on the *plouc* side nearer Spain. I'm more likely to run into him in England or New York than France. But we keep in touch by email. When Macron began his manoeuvres for the presidency, I sent a gossipy email to Andrew explaining why I thought he might win, and how peculiar he was.

Andrew was then chairman of the *Spectator*, in addition to presenting for the BBC, and his response was to suggest to Fraser Nelson, the *Spectator*'s editor, that he take me on as the French political correspondent, writing for the magazine and website. A very grand appointment paying peanuts. Fraser agreed. I have now covered Macron through two presidential elections and non-stop interstitial *magouilles* (fishy moves) that make his reign a golden one for a freelancer.

Many rum coves have ruled France and Macron is amongst the rummiest. I had a feel from the start that there was something pathological about him. The narcissistic personality disorder was in plain sight. I've also never shrugged my shoulders at his marriage to his *lycée* drama teacher, 24 years his senior. Biographer Brenda Maddox taught me always to *cherchez la femme*, and Brigitte is as curious a character as he is. She had three children before her marriage to Macron, which is childless. He's younger than his stepchildren. In some ways he's her fourth child.

There are reasons I'm not invited to Macron's Elysée Palace for cosy chats, like Sophie Pedder, the *Economist* correspondent in Paris, after her magazine depicted Macron walking on water and declared him Europe's saviour. My line is less charitable. A few headlines from my author page at the *Spectator* offer a flavour of my coverage. 'Emmanuel Macron looks shiftier and less likeable by the minute', I wrote in November 2017. 'Macron is the author of his own despair', in December 2024, after he plunged the country into new chaos with yet another tantrum.

I have never met Macron. Living in the Languedoc I'm far from included in the charmed circle of political journalists in France, who in their groupthink bubble are identical to their homologues in London and Washington. It's a club of which I don't wish to be a member, and given how rude I have been about them, they wouldn't want me. But I know people who know Macron and reckon I have better understood him than most, or at least have been willing to go farther than many of my colleagues in Paris, who have covered up his peculiarities much as the White House press covered up the decline of Joe Biden. Deference is a defect in a republican system where the *de facto* head of government is also head of state.

Given my head by *Spectator* editor Fraser Nelson, I didn't have to soften my habitual bare-knuckle approach. A number of my articles were translated into French and republished in *Courier International* magazine. I don't know if Macron has seen them. But someone at the Elysée probably has, so I'm *persona non grata* there. I'm not bothered by my lack of access to the presidential palace. I see Macron much more through the filter of the people in my village. When the Gilets Jaunes movement started in France in late 2018 as a grassroots protest against fuel tax hikes and the rising cost of living, I understood it immediately because the demonstrators in their high-visibility gilets were my neighbours. While journalists in Paris were demonising the demonstrators as thugs and trouble-makers, I was spending time with them on the roundabouts where they'd set up their camps. My Labrador, Ringo, was as ever an icebreaker. I have a soft spot for troublemakers.

Macron has united France against him. But he's been good for me. The *Spectator* can't get enough of him. In July 2024 after he had lost his parliamentary majority after throwing a hissy fit calling unnecessary elections, I opined that he can be very charming in a small group, where it's clear he is the sovereign. But in public he is clumsy and sometimes outrageous. Also, bizarrely, I have noted how he loves to dress up.

At the very start of his presidency, he had himself photographed in a beautifully cut suit, the Legion d'Honneur on his lapel luminous as if lit by a laser, solemnly proceeding through the Hall of Mirrors at Versailles, flanked by the Republican Guard in their extravagant dress uniforms, with drawn swords. It was beautifully photographed, and an extraordinary, boastful image. The French had elected a king, an absolute monarch.

Soon, after brutally sacking the chief of the military to show he was in charge, he moved to establish his authority as commander in chief by visiting a French nuclear submarine and dressing up like a naval officer in a military tunic. A grand spectacle. He arrived in a military helicopter. More recently he took to a khaki sweatshirt to channel Volodymyr Zelenskyy. Macron the warrior. Then it was his Sylvester Stallone tribute, Emmanuel 'Rocky' Balboa Macron, working out with a punch bag in a gym in Paris. The photograph was taken by the official Elysée photographer and the bulgy biceps are rumoured to have been photoshopped in post-production. The stunt is thought to have been Brigitte's idea. Boxing fans were nevertheless unimpressed by his jab.

In the most provocative gesture of them all, he dressed up like Tom Cruise. The very day after the first round of the 2024 National Assembly election, which he had lost, he was parading before the paps in a stylish leather jacket and baseball cap. The Top Gun. Lieutenant Emmanuel 'Maverick' Macron. Brigitte wore Yves Saint Laurent. Macron imagines himself to be Jupiter, king of the gods. I see him as an actor *manqué,* a rampant narcissist.

I doubt that attending Elysée press conferences is necessarily an effective way of covering this presidency. Keeping eyes open to what you see, and not what politicians say, is better. This is another Miller Rule of Journalism. There's no substitute for observation, whether you're covering a presidency or a village fête. I'm now probably getting a little weary of Macron. And I am not thrilled at the prospect of writing about another presidential election. But just like a politician, I'm not ruling it out. Maybe one more rodeo.

More and more, my writing for the *Spectator* has become a potpourri of other subjects—education, food, sexual mores, the fabulous French health system. Health has been an especially fertile ground, for a mostly British audience victims of the NHS.

I have covered the remarkable behaviour of French GPs, who actually answer the phone. And will see you the same day, if necessary. Or tomorrow, if less immediately urgent. I have told of the remarkable private emergency room in Pézenas where I took my wife after she broke a bone in her foot. She was seen by a triage nurse in six minutes, was in radiology in 20, and discharged in one hour. Although private, it's covered by the Sécu social security system, and is the same price as a public hospital. The bill was €19. Lab work? Just show up at the medical laboratory in every French town. Results come the same day over an app.

Then there was my adventure at the big public hospital in Béziers which made me wait two entire days for a temporal biopsy in search of terrifying giant cells that can make you blind. They didn't find any. Clean hospital? Check. Amazing space-age operating theatre? Check. Kind nurses? Check. Free parking? Check.

To be balanced, not everything is perfect in the French system. An aging population, new treatments, all have stressed the Sécu budget to breaking point. The deficit, including pension obligations, is expected to reach €25 billion this year. Not that this is ever visible to most patients. Health spending per capita in France is broadly similar to that in Britain, albeit delivering more bang for the buck.

I have been amused to watch the new British government

promise a digital health service, revolutionising administration and cutting waiting lists. We've had this in France for years. Everything involving health care in France is done with the Carte Vitale card, which you use to show entitlement to treatment. You present this at every health care intervention in France, even at the pharmacy. The Sécu picks up the bill, with a small co-payment from the patient. A visit to the GP costs €8. My operation in Béziers was €59. I pay more to take my dog to the vet.

The stories aren't all serious. I had a bit of a rash on my chest and calves and my GP had a peep at the spots but wasn't sure what she was looking at. '*Bizarre*', she pronounced, not a word you want to hear from a medic. So she made an appointment for me with a dermatologist.

So, everything ran on rails. I presented myself at the dermatology clinic, showed my Carte Vitale, waited an almost outrageous 10 minutes, then the doctor, Marie, put her head around the door and it was show time. Literally, as it transpired.

Others in my cohort will recognise the phenomenon that as we mature, everyone around us doing serious jobs looks younger. Police superintendents, the prime minister, you get the picture. And so it is in medicine. My consultant was young enough to be my daughter, in her mid-thirties at most.

In her office I explained my not enormously interesting medical history and the story of my rash; she asked questions and took notes. 'Right,' she said, pointing to a screened changing area. 'Go there and take your clothes off.' Meaning all of them. I had half expected this but there was a slight twist. In Britain, I recall, they normally give you one of those paper gowns, to preserve a modicum of patient modesty, while the medic examines the body parts in question.

So I go behind the screen, strip to my skin and look for the robe. There isn't one. It's apparently a cost they forgo at the dermatology clinic—along with diversity officers. So I am standing there naked when the doctor appears, looks me up and down with clinical detachment and invites me to lie down on the examination table.

She then proceeds to examine every square centimetre of my body. And I mean every one. I am lying starkers on the table, not a handkerchief to preserve whatever dignity I have remaining, affecting a studied nonchalance, what the French call a *mine de rien,* and staring at the ceiling.

After several minutes of examining me from basement to attic, or soup to nuts, choose what metaphor you want, she seems slightly disappointed that she had found nothing especially interesting. 'It doesn't look as bad as the photos your GP sent me'. She sent me away with a prescription for various lotions and potions, and told me to come back in a month. The bill was €16.

She was kind but not especially chatty. I wanted to ask her what it was like, having a job with a parade of naked people before her all day, but thought the question might be interpreted as pervy, so bit my tongue.

Other than my normal plaudits for the French health system, I am not sure what lessons might be drawn from this experience except that in France, you don't need to wear clean underwear to the doctor, because you won't be wearing any when she examines you.

As was predictable, my efforts to show Britain that there is a demonstrably superior model for health care, have fallen on deaf ears. The new Labour government has embarked on still more reform of 'our' NHS, that will inevitably be as unavailing as all the reforms that have preceded it.

21

COFFEE HOUSE

'More of a cocktail party than a political party'—2024
'It is the folly of too many to mistake the echo of a London coffee-house for
the voice of the kingdom'—Jonathan Swift

When I am in London I like to drop in at the *Spectator* building in
Westminster. The magazine which is no longer just a magazine is in
some ways a throwback and in others is a model for a media business that has positioned itself well for the next chapter, having successfully traversed the great derangement. The *Spectator* is the oldest
continuously published magazine in the world. It seems to be navigating the rapids of today's world with success. It would do better
with me in charge but that's not an option.

The Speccie is based in an eccentric 17th century building at 22,
Old Queen Street, a couple of minutes from the Palace of
Westminster, around the corner from the old MI6 headquarters. It
is not, to be clear, a street reserved for superannuated homosexuals.
Once a grand private residence, it backs onto Birdcage Walk and
Saint James's Park. The spacious private garden is the scene of cel-
ebrated parties, attracting politicians of left and right. Alexander
Chancellor, an editor of the magazine in the seventies, set the tone
when he declared the *Spectator* 'more of a cocktail party than a political party.'

Inside is a warren of stairways and passages, the offices
crammed with computers. Were all this to move to a floor of a
modern office block, the magic would surely disappear. There's no
room even for cubicles, the desks are just jammed together. A bit

like the newsroom at the *Michigan Daily*, a bit like the *Communications Daily* townhouse in Washington. Freddy Gray, the deputy editor, has the privilege of an office. The bad news is that it would better serve as a broom closet. The new editor Michael Gove has a slightly more salubrious space. I stopped by recently for the weekly editorial conference. There were no cocktails. I left optimistic. I hadn't previously known Gove, but he ticked some boxes. He reminded me of Andrew Neil in conference. He has a daybook on his knee and notes everything. He has a good memory and can quote poetry. It's very hard to forgive him for collaborating when in Boris Johnson's government with the disastrous Covid lockdowns and I'm not convinced by his explanations. He gets a lot of credit for his attack on the education blob, although his good work is being rapidly undone by his successor Bridget Phillipson. Gove started as a journalist and was a good one before getting diverted into politics and has now returned to the fold. I am willing to forgive him his transgressions as a politician given that I myself swerved down this path, although Michael colossally more significantly.

Why do journalists love to write for the *Spectator*? There's never a hard 'line to take.' You can write anything you like as long as it's well argued with extra points for mischievousness. There are commentators below the line convinced that Gove has secretly decreed a tilt to the left. If this is true I have not been informed.

The magazine is Tory, in an obsolete meaning of the word, conservative with a small 'c'. Fraser Nelson[54] was the editor for 15 years until he was replaced or quit or was fired or just decided to call it a day—I don't know—after the magazine's sale in 2024 to Sir Paul Marshall for £100 million pounds. Sir Paul has his fingers in GB News and *Unherd* and has ambitions to be a media magnate on the right. Fraser has left an indelible stamp. He was a terrific editor, hiring an eccentric cohort of assistants, uninterested in conformity. He was the patron of the resume-free job application. More interested in what a candidate can do, than the academics. He has subsequently gone to *The Times* as a columnist. Though a centrist by instinct, he was naughty, an essential quality for an editor. He doubled the circulation during his tenure and developed a hybrid strategy with chairman Andrew Neil that was neither 'digital first' nor afraid of paper, but seeing the physical magazine, printed on quality paper, as something special. The *Coffee House* blog is an organic development of the magazine's reputation for contrariness and idiosyncrasy. The pair also launched a suite of podcasts and a YouTube channel. Spectator TV is the exact opposite of mainstream political shows. Guests are not constantly interrupted by hyper-coiffed, vain presenters.

Coffee House is aptly named because it is a tribute to London's coffee houses in the 17th and 18th centuries, which were salons for journalists, writers, and intellectuals. These establishments were more than just places to drink coffee, but vibrant hubs for news exchange, debate, political discussion and sedition. Many of the first newspapers and periodicals were conceived, written, and distributed in these coffee houses.

The blog reflects exactly this tradition, adapted to a new age. Much but not all of it of it is written by freelancers like me, who are paid a pittance. There's also an active below the line community. *Spectator* subscribers comment mostly civilly and intelligently; it is a more congenial space than the imbecilic comments found elsewhere below the line. I think the *Spectator* could do more to cultivate its community and have suggested this to Michael Gove.

The print magazine itself is not neglected but lavished with attention, always with a provocative cover story, with witty columns and unexpected features. Illustrious names grace its pages. Lionel Shriver, Rod Liddle, Douglas Murray, amongst others. It's strong on politics, arts, the economy, but a bit weak on business. It could do more to compete with the *Economist* if it were to address the world of enterprise with the same no-prisoners-taken attitude it has for politics.

It's worth toiling for the miserable checks because writing for the *Spectator* is so much fun. Many of the contributors are seasoned veterans. I have written hundreds of stories for Coffee House, and many for the magazine. I'm not on staff, am very rarely there, but when I visit, can tell it's a good place to work. Richard Branson once told me the secret to an effective enterprise is a happy staff. And Old Queen Street is happy. It's a fantastic platform for late-career freelancers like me. The editors don't cross out all the jokes. Everyone who matters reads your stuff, including all the other journalists.

Charles Moore, the biographer of Margaret Thatcher, a former editor and since 2024 the chairman of the magazine, tells a wonderful story about Frank Johnson, a former editor, opera lover, sketch-writer extraordinaire and by origin a working-class journalist, incidentally. In his final years he was our neighbour in a nearby village here in France.

In the 1950s, boys in his Shoreditch secondary school, Frank among them, were recruited to fill the crowds on stage at the Royal Opera House, being urchins in numerous productions and screaming dwarves in *Das Rheingold*. In 1957, Frank and one other boy were called in for *Norma* to be the heroine's two children whom she decides to stab to death, but then relents, 'opting instead for a duet with a mezzo-soprano'. Callas was Norma. Frank forgot most of the evening but 'I could not forget that when Callas bore down on us with knife, her nostrils flared; that when, dropping the knife, she repentantly clasped us to her bosom, her perfume smelt like that of an aunt who was always kissing me; and that… there penetrated, into my left eye, the top of the diva's right breast, which partnership remained throughout the subsequent duet'. In that eye, Frank felt 'the most distinct pain as that voice of myth and legend rose and fell. In the other eye, all I could see was the exit sign at the far corner of the gallery. At the second performance, I ducked and secured a central portion of the diva's bosom'. 'There are few men', Frank concluded, 'who can truthfully say that their eye made contact with the right nipple of Maria Callas.' It's storytelling like this that gives the *Spectator* its peculiarity.

The *Spectator* also has a skeleton in its closet. Another former editor is Boris Johnson, fired by Andrew Neil when he arrived in 2005 because he was completely terrible, trying to do the job while simultaneously a Conservative MP, conducting an extra-marital affair with the columnist Petronella Wyatt and publishing an ill-judged editorial slagging off the people of Liverpool, although I had a certain sympathy with his analysis. Johnson was an inventive journalist, meaning he made stuff up. In an earlier manifestation as the Brussels correspondent of the *Daily Telegraph*, he reported that the EU was to introduce a common European condom. It was one of those stories too good not to check. So I did check it, and it wasn't true. But he once bought me lunch in Brussels and the conversation was good. The notion that he would one day be prime minister was unimaginable, except perhaps for him.

22.

MY WAR WITH THE BBC

...and Failure to Destroy It—Thus far
'The BBC is a mixture of a girls' school and a lunatic asylum'
—attributed to George Orwell

I pause the narrative to settle a feud. Mrs Miller says I am a bore on this subject, although I suspect she silently agrees with me. If you don't much care about the BBC, skim or skip to the next chapter. Otherwise join me, the angry journalist wearing my media correspondent's hat, in what I hope might stand as my definitive denunciation of this grotesque institution. I have spent decades fruitlessly trying to bring down this institution. I don't expect this *hurlement* will change anything.

Start from first principles. The never-asked question is, what is public broadcasting? It's not the BBC, that's for sure. The public is served what the BBC considers good for it. The BBC is a state broadcaster, an anachronism captured by a groupthink elite that poisons public discourse with its messaging. Even shows like Dr Who have been taken over by the agenda.[55] It is gratifying to see in 2025 that the BBC has never been under such attack. But I am not optimistic the pressure will produce the necessary changes.

My unfinished business with the BBC is its destruction. I used to be more charitable and thought it might be reformed. That's impossible. I thought maybe it could respect diversity of opinion as well as DEI. That was wrong, too. I've never liked being told what to think and the BBC's patronising voice and superior airs have enraged me as much as the grotesque financing and governance of this ideological apparatus.

From the day I started covering the BBC as media correspondent of *The Times*, my instincts told me that this was a sinister organisation, self-regarding, dissembling in its own defence, terrible value for money, peddling its own hidden agendas, with zero direct accountability to its captive customers. Yet worshipped, apparently, as the Best of British, like the equally awful National Health Service.

I am not the first and far from the most celebrated journalist to have noticed the malignity of the BBC. George Orwell worked there and walked out, describing the work as 'soul destroying'. He used the BBC in the novel *1984* as the model for the Ministry of Truth. How he would have laughed at the recent establishment of BBC Verify,[56] which quite openly proclaims its goal to be the Arbiter of Truth.

My first point of contact with the BBC when I was at *The Times* was the Press Office at Broadcasting House. You enter BH under a stone carving declaring 'Nation Shall Speak Unto Nation', the mission statement of the first director general, Sir John Reith. A lofty ambition. Also, although I didn't twig it at the time, there was a suggestive statue of Prospero and Ariel over the entrance, by Sir Eric Gill, who, it was later revealed, sexually abused his daughters. An apt if unwitting welcome to an organisation with a rich history of paedophilia. Upstairs, I met a very strange man, the chief press officer, who flirted with me and called me Petal, so read into that what you will. Creepy.

From my first press conference appearance as the newly minted media correspondent of *The Times*, already a pariah paper in their minds, they knew I wasn't their friend.

The then director general Alastair Milne had invited the media correspondents to Broadcasting House for the presentation of the corporation's Annual Report and Accounts. It was a big annual set-piece event where the director boasted of success and promised more to come. The media hacks consisting of national newspaper correspondents like me, the trade press, and a vast number of the BBC's own journalists, from various programmes, sat obediently through this exegesis. I was incredulous. This was nothing like the rowdy press conferences I remembered from Washington. That was blood sport This was cringy, pathetic. Everyone sat like numpties as Milne delivered his speech and I sat at the back, reading the accounts.

Eventually, he finished and we were invited to ask questions. I stood up and asked if these were the only numbers available, if there were some actual accounts, because the numbers I was reading in the Annual Accounts before me made no sense at all. Milne was furious and the other journalists squirmed uncomfortably. Brenda Maddox who was there for the *Telegraph* warned me afterwards, 'This isn't Washington. If you behave like that nobody will talk to you.' But the accounts were just as dodgy as I had suspected. The deeper you look, the murkier it gets.

The fish rots from the head. The governance of the BBC, throughout endless shuffling of the deckchairs, has remained opaque and deficient. The weakness of BBC governance is plain to see in its failures of what is now called safeguarding. Retrospectively I now recognise that the chief press officer's pass at me was a sign of the culture. We have since learned that abuse permeated the establishment from basement to attic, while the management concerned itself with coverup, not accountability.

Sacred BBC 'personalities' like the odious Jimmy Savile, knighted by Thatcher in 1990, were cosseted and protected for decades. Savile was not an aberration. Rolf Harris the TV artist, Stuart Hall (It's a Knockout), Huw Edwards (news presenter) also feature in the gallery of sex criminals harboured by the BBC. In 2025, more cases are pending. There are many others that are known and undoubtedly still more undiscovered, as not all allegations become public.

The abject failures of BBC governance on abuse also characterise its failure to protect the BBC's core mission of impartiality. On environmentalism, the BBC no longer even pretends. Diversity, equity and inclusion permeate its programmes, but diversity of opinion is not a feature. When the BBC does put up an alternative opinion, it tends to choose the looniest and most extreme spokesman.

At the *Sunday Times* I prosecuted a lengthy struggle against the BBC. Andrew Neil was for a no-holds-barred approach to all the broadcasters. But later, John Witherow's heart wasn't really in it. When I refused to pay the licence fee, claiming it was a violation of my rights under the European Convention on Human Rights, he wouldn't support me. I was subsequently convicted at Guildford District Court and fined £150. Murdoch loathed the BBC but it was frankly against his commercial interests to have it launch a competitive subscription platform. I was allowed to demand its liquidation in my columns but not in the Leader, which I authored frequently. I nevertheless was permitted by Witherow to argue that the licence fee is the problem, not the solution.

Lord Thomson of Fleet, the first chairman of the Independent Broadcasting Authority, said the TV licence was a criminalisation of female poverty. That's because the TV licence 'inspectors', who dressed in blue jackets and cosplay policemen, have their happiest hunting grounds on poor council estates, preying on single mothers who were already struggling to cope, and dragging them to court. Most are summarily fined, have no legal representation and a few even end up in jail, after defaulting on fines. A truly hideous and disgusting system in which anyone owning a TV set is a criminal until they pay the licence fee. I went to Croydon magistrates court for the *Sunday Times* to observe a TV licence docket in which more than 100 undefended women were summarily convicted. This is how the BBC treats viewers.

Andrew Neil has for four decades criticised the BBC and other broadcasters for hostility to business and enterprise. There's still no serious business coverage on the BBC, because the culture of the BBC is inherently hostile to enterprise. Because everyone there is on the public payroll and it doesn't matter what the customers think. The BBC's sympathies can never be for Mr Patel the shopkeeper or Tesco. They are for those like themselves. The civil service. The

NHS. The universities. Local authorities. Foundations. NGOs. The groupthink at the BBC is consistent with the opinion of everyone in the subsidiariat.

The BBC is complained about by right and left and claims this proves its impartiality. But this is sophistry. It is not disputable that the BBC is Greta Thunberg on climate and energy, not so hot on Israel,[57] fanatical on racial and gender diversity, obsessed with drag queens, unlimited in its own self-regard, and deliberately misleading on 'our' NHS. It's in love with itself. Even its quiz shows include an obligatory question about the BBC, lest we forget to honour it at every opportunity. Even its soaps have an agenda. Casualty and Holby City glorify the NHS; EastEnders worships multiculturalism. Its news is blatantly partisan and incompetent. Its political correspondents obsessed about who ate cake in Downing Street during the Covid lockdown. They didn't question the wisdom of the lockdown or the vaccination of children supposedly to protect adults, or why it was that NHS staff were making Tiktok videos in empty hospitals.

The ballyhooed World Service is often cited as a reason why we need the BBC. The first problem with this argument is the difficulty of knowing if the World Service with its obsolete short wave radio network and now its web pages and podcasts, is really projecting British power, as claimed, or is just irrelevant, lost in the clamour. The evidence is at best anecdotal and unconvincing. It is likely that the World Service is merely a gigantic waste of money.

A second reason is that the language services have for decades been infested with spies[58] and ideologues, although this has never to my knowledge been properly investigated. It is doubtful that senior BBC management understands a word of what's being broadcast in Chinese.

I have tried and failed to raise the question, what even is public broadcasting? Programming in the public interest, or programming that the public finds interesting? Maybe the public wants public broadcasting or maybe not. Why not find out? Let competition bloom. Start with another question assiduously avoided. Why is there only one BBC? Why is one monolithic organisation in receipt of the entirety of the licence fee? Why not cut parts loose? Let Radio Four operate on its own. Shut down the banshees of Radio Two. Let others use its frequencies. There are potentially scores of alternative providers of public broadcasting, be they trusts, universities, non-profits, cooperatives—whatever the public wants, let it pay for, voluntarily.

The shibboleth of the licence fee may not survive. The promised forthcoming Labour 'reform' of the BBC might end up tinkering with the funding mechanism, possibly financing the BBC entirely with tax money.[59] A terrible idea. In what will be spun as a 'major' concession, the BBC will promise to migrate more programmes to its online iPlayer platform to increase the share of its income it generates for itself, to live within its means. Blahblahblah. I'm a cynic but it looks to me as if the BBC is cruising into a second life. Its charter will surely be renewed and it will continue to feed at the public teat.

It is astonishing in any case that we are still talking about a license fee, and that there are still those who defend it.

A brief history. It was introduced 102 years ago after the Great War. The Home Office feared the dangerous security consequences of the new medium that had emerged from wartime technical advances in wireless. In 1923 the first wireless (radio) licence was introduced, costing 10 shillings. By the end of the year, 200,000 licences were sold.

By 1928 the number of licences had risen to 2.5 million. The BBC was stuffed with cash, off and running. And 100 years later, it is still claiming a charge on the public for programmes viewers do not choose to watch, using frequencies that could be much better employed in other services such as new generations of mobile devices. The BBC is not just a fat pig, it's a road hog.[60]

The TV licence currently costs £174.50 per year and is required whether you watch the BBC or not. More than 150,000 people a year have been prosecuted and summarily convicted. The BBC has insisted that the licence fee represents good value for money but if this is the case, why is it not a voluntary subscription? If it was good value, millions would surely subscribe. In 2024, Netflix had roughly 17 million subscribers in Britain, paying as little as £6.99 per month (£83.88 per year) for the ad supported version of the service. YouTube, Amazon and Apple all have millions of UK subscribers and all are cheaper than the BBC.

Supporters of the BBC licence fee are not just the *Guardian* and most of the rest of the media. They include the former British Prime Minister David Cameron. Indeed the Tories have vociferously supported the BBC for years, much as they genuflect to 'our NHS.' When Cameron was canvassing candidates for the then-vacant job of BBC chairman, it was on the sole condition that they would defend the licence fee. Some refused.

The BBC Board comprises fourteen members, including both non-executive and executive directors. There are four executive members including the director-general Tim Davie. Five non-executive members including the chairman are appointed by the government, meaning the patronage of the prime minister. The current chairman is Samir Shah, a quintessential member of the broadcasting elite. Five additional NEDs are elected by the BBC Board itself through its nominations committee. This bizarre arrangement supposedly represents the public interest. In practice the BBC management runs the show.

The refusal to confront the contradictions of the BBC has left it intact as new technology has made it less relevant with every passing month. The BBC is facing a demographic time bomb. In 2022, only one in 20 young adults watched BBC TV live daily. In 2023, fewer than half of 16-24-year-olds in the UK regularly watched it. Yoof is spending more time with video-sharing platforms like YouTube and TikTok.

My doubts about the BBC accounts expressed to general opprobrium so long ago have not been resolved to this day. Deconstructing the BBC's accounts is akin to the complex forensic investigation of Enron, the American energy trader that collapsed in 2001 as a result of massive fraud.

David Elstein, a former senior executive at Thames Television and now a media critic, accuses the BBC of blatant accounting deceptions. The most obvious of the BBC's fantasy claims, says Elstein, is that expenditure on overheads only takes up 5 per cent of its licence fee income. 'Anyone who has worked in broadcasting will know, there are two types of outgoings: the cost of programmes… and everything else. Typically, these will constitute around 40 per cent of all expenditure.'

Until 2024, there was one other set of data in the annual reports that gave a clue to the balance between content creation and overheads, says Elstein. In the small print, there was a breakdown of the 15,885 staff. Just 4825 were classified as working on content and 11,060 (or 70 per cent) on support. In a previous report, out of 19,866 staff, 10,255 (52 per cent) were classified as support, administration, engineering, sales, marketing and communications.

'It (is) simply impossible for the 5 per cent figure to be correct,' Elstein says. But it's worse than that.

The total income for the BBC in 2021/22 was £5.3 billion, with the TV licence fee contributing around £3.8 billion, which accounts for approximately 71% of the BBC's total income. The rest comes from its commercial activities and grants from the likes of the EU and foundations, including the Bill Gates foundation. U.S government funding of the BBC supposedly for the training of journalists has been terminated by the Trump administration.

Where does this money go? In 2013, it was reported that the BBC decided to use £740 million of licence fee payers' money to address a 'black hole' in its pension fund. This amount was intended to cover a deficit that had grown to £2 billion. This means that each licence fee payer was indirectly contributing roughly £7.36 annually to pay pensions to BBC retirees.

The enormous pay checks of BBC stars are but a rounding error compared to the cost of the pensions. But just for fun, here's the list of the best-paid BBC stars:

- Gary Lineker—£1.35 million. Although his gravy train is now coming to an end, the retired football star turned football pundit, social justice warrior and ambassador for potato crisps, has been the top earner for several consecutive years, primarily for his work on Match of the Day, Sports Personality Of The Year, and other sports coverage.

- Zoe Ball—£950,000. The host of the Radio 2 breakfast show. I've never listened but is this really public service broadcasting? She's now gone.

- Alan Shearer—another footballer on the payroll, has earned up to £445,000 a year.

- Huw Edwards—The latest BBC sex scandal protagonist. He liked exchanging naked pictures with boys and was convicted on three counts of making indecent images of children. His salary increased by £40,000 to £475,000 before he left the BBC on medical advice in April 2024.

Other notable high earners include Fiona Bruce, whose salary is reported between £405,000 and £409, 999, Stephen Nolan, between £405,000 and £409,999, Greg James, the Radio One presenter, between £390,000 and £394,000. I confess, I've never heard of some of these people.

This is only the tip of the iceberg. The BBC only discloses salaries for stars paid directly by the corporation, not those paid through independent production companies or BBC Studios, its commercial arm. This means well-known presenters like regime satirist Ian Hislop, Claudia Winkleman, Michael McIntyre, and Graham Norton do not appear on this list as their earnings come through different channels.

Also undisclosed are the appearance fees the BBC pays tame politicians and journalists. Some of the stoutest defenders of the BBC in British media are also amongst those who will have been participating in the most lucrative BBC gigs. But this isn't disclosed. What has Polly Toynbee of the *Guardian*, stout defender of the BBC, a constant presence on BBC airwaves, collected in BBC appearance fees? I don't know. She should tell us.

In 2025, the BBC was lobbying the government to allow it to collect licence fees from viewers who watch only streaming services like Netflix. The BBC demand illustrates its Olympian detachment from any idea that viewers should make their own choices.

The corporation speaks in babble, as if its captive licence payers are imbeciles. 'We want everyone to get value for money from the BBC which is why we are focused on delivering what audiences want from us—trusted news, the best home-grown storytelling and the moments that bring us together,' it boasts. The BBC is delivering on none of these.

The corporation now promises to launch 'our biggest ever public engagement exercise so audiences can help drive and shape what they want from a universal and independent BBC in the future.' This is code for a massively expensive information campaign to persuade us of its virtues. 'We look forward to engaging with government on the next charter and securing the long-term future of the BBC,' says the BBC, knowing it is knocking at an open door in Whitehall.

Andrew Neil, who I always thought way too generous to the BBC, having supported the licence fee in the past, but who may now be seeing the error of his ways, points out that the BBC has not created a new TV hit for five years, citing data from the National Audit Office. Its commercial division makes most of its money from old shows that were first released decades ago. Of the BBC's 10 most profitable shows last year, only one—a 'soft drama' series from 2019—was created by BBC Studios, while three were bought from rival producers.

Shovelling money to a cultural elite in the name of universality is a nonsense in an era when anyone can broadcast to the world from their spare bedroom.

It's astonishing to me that the BBC still exists and will soon celebrate its 100th birthday, although I will not be invited to the party. Forensic accountants should raid Broadcasting House. The BBC's survival remains my greatest failure as a journalist.

23

BELIEVERS

'Trust me, I'm a journalist.'—Fleet Street adage.

The story that journalists don't want to acknowledge is that confidence in journalism has collapsed. It's unlikely to be true that journalists themselves are entirely responsible. Global digitisation of media has spawned a cacophony in which trained journalists have been overwhelmed by amateurs. But journalists are not blameless. Journalism has lost specialists, journalists who knew something about their subject. And many of those who are still supposedly specialists, haven't a clue. It's egregious. The *Daily Mail* used to have an aviation correspondent. It recently referred to an antique Spitfire as a jet. Many of the current specialists at *The Times* are embarrassing. The media have lost authority because they are less authoritative.

But I don't think that's all. Journalists have lost touch with their readers. They have become a disconnected, often hereditary elite. It's rare that journalists have contact with anyone unlike themselves. When you see a pack of journalists, they talk to each other.

I am reluctant to agree with Noam Chomsky, a celebrated writer of the left, but it's a strong point well made that, 'If you are working 50 hours a week in a factory, you don't have time to read 10 newspapers a day.' Which suggests that the one that they do read should try harder.

There has always been a Cathar-like dualism in our profession, glory tempered with ignobility. Yet public trust in journalism was once relatively high. In America, before the internet, between 68% and 72% according to Gallup. By the late 1990s to early 2000s, trust began to wane, hovering around 51% to 55%. Post 2004, as the internet arrived, trust in the media saw a significant drop, with levels not rising above 47% since 2005. By 2020, only 40% of Americans expressed 'a great deal' or 'a fair amount' of trust in the media to report the news fully, accurately, and fairly. Trust has continued to decline, reaching historic lows. According to various polls, including those from Gallup, only about 32% of Americans express confidence in the media's ability to report news in an unbiased manner.

This isn't an exclusively American phenomenon. Multiple polls indicate a decline in trust in the news media across Europe. The Reuters Institute digital news report in 2023 found only 30% of respondents expressing trust in media. Trust in UK news media has fallen from 51% in 2015 to just 34% in 2022. By 2022, 46% of UK respondents reported actively avoiding news, a figure nearly double that of 2017.

How about the hereditary class of journalists decried by Julie Burchill that has crowded out working-class talent such as former *Spectator* editor Frank Johnson? There's an alibi for elite journalists that nobody's credibility could survive the clamour of the internet. But the case against is the recent American election campaign, which saw hyper partisan elite media undermine their own credibility by praising Joe Biden until it became impossible to conceal his infirmity.

'Then, overnight, the media pack tore him apart for being too old and infirm, memory-holing the fact that they had spent the past three years assailing anyone who questioned the lie that he was sharp as a tack,' wrote Bari Weiss in in her blog, the *Free Press*.

'Attacks on Trump were so bizarrely strident, and at the same time so ritualised, that they attained the aspect of parody if not wit,' she observed. The *Atlantic,* owned by Laurene Jobs, a progressive activist and the widow of Steve Jobs, ran a piece titled 'Trump is Speaking like Hitler, Stalin and Mussolini.' Trump was meanwhile cooking french fries at a McDonald's in Pennsylvania.

I put this to Eugene Robinson, a friend, *Washington Post* columnist, TV commentator and *Michigan Daily* contemporary risen to the high table of Washington punditry. He is a quintessential left-lane establishment journalist but honest and a good mate.

'Up to a point,' he defends. 'The *Free Press*, as usual, allows its glee at the misfortune of traditional media to outrun the more pedestrian facts. Which, to be sure, are dire enough without embellishment. The *Post* lost $77 million in 2023, not because of subscription and readership trends (which were bad and would have created a smaller loss) but because our then-publisher went on an insane hiring spree, based on revenue projections that any competent executive would have seen as hallucinatory. Biden in mid-2023 was not the senile dotard of mid-2024, and I can attest to that personally; he was too old to run again, certainly, but he was not incompetent.'

So, there may be two sides to the story, but the legacy media, the mainstream media, the corporate media, whatever it is called, has never been so vulnerable nor the consumers of news so unconvinced. And journalists who try to tell readers what to think must bear much blame.

We journalists need to ask ourselves a hard question. Why don't our readers, viewers and listeners believe us? And the answer is that public has reacted predictably at being told things are true when they obviously are not. The media has been challenged as never before.

Like him or not, Donald Trump leveraged disgust with the so-called 'mainstream media' into a major if unquantifiable contributor to his victory. Campaigning under what could have been a banner of #youdonthatethemediaenough, Trump wasn't intimidated by the so-called mainstream (or 'lamestream') media. He made the media a campaign issue. Trump suggested that networks like MSNBC and NBC's parent company, Comcast, should be investigated for treason, and filed a $10 billion suit against CBS for doctoring an interview with his opponent Kamala Harris. But the public didn't need Trump to tell them that they were being fed bollocks. During riots provoked by the death of the drug-addled George Floyd in Minnesota, provoking the Black Lives Matter movement, a CNN reporter posed in front of a burning city block and pronounced the riots to be 'mostly peaceful.' This imbecility was seen over and over again by millions on social platforms.

The Trump wave is surely now arriving in Europe and beyond, where populist politicians are starting to directly challenge journalists from the mainstream. It's an open goal.

An obsession with racism and equity, transgenderism and pronouns has led many journalists into a place where they almost seem to relish insulting their readers, viewers and listeners. Government-subsidised media in Canada shredded their own credibility with hysterical reporting of alleged graves at indigenous schools in the west, supposedly containing the remains of abused and neglected children. Words like genocide were employed. Yet no human remains have been found. Those who suggest the entire story was concocted have been accused of denialism. In Australia the media piled in behind the Voice referendum on indigenous rights, only for the voters to reject it. When footballers took the knee in Britain to support Black Lives Matter, the broadcasters were forced to censor shots of booing fans.

The media was at its worst when the pandemic rocked up. Medically-illiterate political correspondents took over what editors treated as a political story. They behaved like a gallery of monkeys, demanding that politicians lockdown harder and faster, while ignoring lockdown rules themselves, like Kay Burley of Sky News. The media, along with much of the medical establishment and politicians, panicked. The press conferences were like bear baiting as scientifically illiterate political reporters demanded harsher measures.

Mainstream media actively suppressed dissident narratives that challenged official policies. Social media companies censored posts questioning lockdowns, vaccine mandates, or alternative treatments, often labelling them as misinformation. Scientists and doctors voicing contrary views faced deplatforming, job losses, or reputational attacks. The media didn't just fail, it colluded in an outcome in which children were deprived of education, normal health services were suspended and catastrophic economic damage ensued.

It would help boost confidence if the media stopped peddling pathetic lies. Its hatred for Donald Trump has deranged it. But right-wing media are often just as detached from reality as the left-wing flavour. 'At Oval Office, Musk Makes Broad Claims of Federal Fraud Without Proof,' thundered the *New York Times* in February 2025. But the federal government itself, when Biden was president, estimated fraud at $233–$521 billion.

Do elite journalists take us for fools?

24

THE TRILLION DOLLAR BRAIN

Whenever it is said that something is clear it almost certainly is not

My *Michigan Daily* contemporary the legendary political pundit Walter Shapiro used to wryly observe that every useful argument made three points, A, B and 3. Which covers the argument I am now going to make that the journalism and 'the news' as we knew them are no longer possible. It's an argument in three movements.

The first is the role of artificial intelligence, a mortal threat to journalism, which seems to be receiving the same insouciant inattention from many media owners as the previous earthquake of the internet. A brief revisitation of how we got here.

It was my cohort of journalists that first figured out the lethal peril facing newspapers but we were not quite senior enough to make a difference. Our elders mostly had their heads in the sand. Sara Fitzgerald, another in the mafia of *Michigan Daily* alumni, struggled in vain to persuade the *Washington Post* to wake up.

'My theory is that at the point when the newspaper industry needed to reinvent themselves, they were too fat and sassy (at the height of their circulation) to do it. The *Post*, the [*New York*] *Times*, *USA Today* and every chain felt THEY could be the national paper,' she recollects.

'The *Post* still believed that its perspective was more valuable than the average reader's. Around 1994 it was still fretting over which online service had the most paper-like interface.'

Her experience at the *Post* echoes my own at News Corporation. It was mostly a losing battle to get senior management to pay attention and develop a strategy.

Will the media owners pay attention this time, as they did not before? Will they be crushed by AI? General Chuck Yeager warned of technical systems too complicated to be understood. What happens when Facebook, TikTok, Instagram and X are entirely driven by AI? Are we anymore autonomous humans or just another brick in the wall, manipulated in ways we can't possibly understand? We have created an information ecology so vast as to be incomprehensible.

The product of an AI search comes with a list of ingredients, if you ask nicely. Harmful additives and excessive processing contaminate the results. AI is simultaneously a cornucopia of plenty and a vast wasteland. Some of it is authoritative, worthy and credible, much is not. But one consequence is that the hack with his press card in the brim of his trilby is gone.

Journalism is no more the rough and ready trade described by Ben Hecht and Evelyn Waugh. Nor will elite journalists necessarily rule the roost much longer. The influence of journalists was fading even before the arrival of AI. There are no more Apples or Broders.

And now, the trillion dollar brain arrives to finish them off.

The tsunami drowning the news in sludge was triggered, inevitably, from convergence, the extraordinary power of colliding technologies. I began to understand this in Washington covering telecommunications, space technology and media. When satellites and cable converged in America to shatter the complacent broadcast industry, the convergence of technologies meant that 1+1 could effectively equal 3. The power of convergence was shown more recently when the internet met digital video, resulting in streaming, which now renders obsolete all assumptions about broadcasting. And coming is the convergence of AI with everything, including journalism. This will be the biggest bang of all.

I could have spent a lot of time imagining all the implications for journalism of artificial intelligence. But I asked Elon Musk's

Grok AI to do it for me. Grok is like a diligent research assistant who sometimes gets the wrong end of the stick. Its answer on AI is comprehensive and revealing simply because it's bloodless. A robot's eye view of our robotic future. I reproduce Grok's answer below noting that it is witless. Sneer if you like. It's only going to get more sophisticated. But it hits the key points.

Opportunities for Journalism with AI

AI offers numerous tools and capabilities that can enhance journalistic practices:

Automation of Routine Tasks

—AI can automate repetitive tasks such as data analysis, fact-checking, and transcription of interviews. This allows journalists to focus on more creative and investigative aspects of their work. For example, AI tools can quickly analyze large datasets to identify trends or anomalies, which is particularly useful for investigative journalism.

Enhanced Storytelling

—AI can assist in creating more engaging and personalized content. For instance, natural language generation (NLG) tools can produce summaries or reports tailored to specific audiences.

—Visual storytelling can be enhanced through AI-generated infographics or interactive media (though I must note I cannot generate charts or diagrams specifically).

Real-Time Reporting

—AI can process and analyze real-time data from social media, news wires, and other sources to provide up-to-the-minute coverage of events. This can be particularly valuable for breaking news situations.

Improved Accessibility

—AI-driven translation and transcription tools can make journalism more accessible to diverse audiences, including those who speak different languages or have disabilities.

Audience Engagement

—AI can help newsrooms better understand their audiences

through data analytics, enabling them to tailor content to reader preferences and behaviors.

Challenges and Risks of AI in Journalism

While AI presents opportunities, it also introduces significant challenges that could further erode public trust in media:

Misinformation and Deepfakes

—AI can be used to create highly convincing fake news, deepfake videos, or manipulated audio. This exacerbates the existing problem of misinformation and makes it harder for audiences to discern credible journalism from fabricated content.

—Journalists will need to develop new tools and skills to verify AI-generated content, which could strain resources.

Bias in AI Systems

—AI systems are trained on historical data, which may contain biases. If these biases are not addressed, AI could perpetuate or even amplify existing inequalities in media coverage.

—For example, AI tools used for audience targeting might prioritize sensationalist stories over substantive reporting, reinforcing clickbait culture.

Job Displacement

—Automation of tasks like writing sports recaps or financial reports could lead to job losses in newsrooms, particularly for entry-level journalists. This raises concerns about the diversity of voices in journalism and the loss of human nuance in storytelling.

Erosion of Editorial Independence

—As news organizations increasingly rely on AI-driven analytics to determine what stories to cover, there is a risk that editorial decisions will be overly influenced by algorithms designed to maximize engagement rather than public interest.

—This could deepen the existing trust deficit if audiences perceive journalism as driven by profit motives rather than truth.

Ethical Concerns

—The use of AI in journalism raises ethical questions, such as the transparency of AI-generated content. Should audiences always be informed when a story has been written or edited by an AI? Lack of clarity could further damage trust.

The Trust Deficit and AI's Role

Public confidence in mainstream media is already low due to perceived biases, sensationalism, and the influence of corporate or political interests. AI could either help rebuild trust or exacerbate the problem:

Rebuilding Trust

—AI can be used to enhance transparency. For instance, news organizations could use AI to provide detailed source verification or to explain editorial decisions to their audiences.

—Fact-checking powered by AI can help combat misinformation, positioning credible journalism as a bulwark against fake news.

Exacerbating Distrust

—If audiences perceive AI as a tool for manipulation or cost-cutting rather than quality improvement, trust could further erode.

—The increasing prevalence of AI-generated content might lead some to question the authenticity of all media, even when produced by humans.

Obviously this is a cold, machine-written text, but it touches on the salient points, including a scenario in which journalists are replaced with robots. What role will there be for journalists when customised reports refreshed in real time are there for the asking? AI is coming for journalism.

I am a hard user of AI as a virtual assistant. I know it makes stuff up. I try to frame questions carefully, to demand sources, to challenge ridiculous answers. AI has saved me literally weeks of research and factchecking. It's an indefatigable if somewhat charmless and autistic researcher.

But it has sinister qualities. The AI engines, which are rapidly becoming the prime vector for search in preference to traditional search engines like Google and Bing, have a point of view. AI plays by some transparent rules to avoid offense, and is blatantly censored. There are the nudging phrases. The refusal to go places. They all censor, ignore and evade awkward facts—they just differ as to what kind of things they find neuralgic, depending on the culture that created them, as my colleague Sean Thomas wrote in the Spectator in January 2025.

The Chinese AI engine DeepSeek is at least honest, admitting it can't answer questions about the 1989 Tiananmen Square massacre and the political status of Taiwan.

Western AIs censor in other, subtler ways. The American market-leading AI engines are simply sneaky.

Wrote Thomas, 'Try asking an American bot like ChatGPT or Claude about anything remotely problematic in regard to race, gender or crime. You will get evasive answers, screeds of weird diversion, or sometimes downright lies.'

Or ask ChatGPT about the horribly thorny question of 'race, genetics and IQ'. 'It lurched into a spasm of unease and then began a long lecture about nutrition, poverty and educational differences—all quite worthy and correct but not actually an answer to the question,' Thomas wrote. Ask Claude for the positives of British colonialism, because despite its many horrors there are of course some, and it will reply that doing so 'could minimize the profound harms and intergenerational trauma inflicted on colonized people.' Google's Gemini—increasingly a contender on the AI leaderboards—is one of the worst. When Gemini relaunched early last year, it insisted on making half of the American Founding Fathers black. This isn't so much censorship as an agenda.

In southern France they say wine reflects the character of its maker. And the character of AI is conditioned by the mores of those developing it. Who are these people? I have yet to meet an AI that I trust, but how much time is left before AI-powered media lays waste to much of today's journalism? For the worker ants, the hacks in the trenches, young journalists entering the workforce, the bell tolls. The competition is no longer the person at the next desk but a data centre cooled by a glacier in Iceland.

Maybe this isn't entirely undesirable.

AI can do a reasonable job at that old-fashioned just-the-facts objectivity. The school lunch menu. The police blotter. He said, she said. The grist of the reporting that is dull but useful. A style of synthetic journalism-like content that will rock no boats but might nevertheless find a market. AI text is still rather boring to read. There's a metallic tone to it. And none of the current AI offerings are yet fully integrating images, videos and deeper links.

I asked ChatGPT to produce the front page of a newspaper with the day's news. After five attempts, it came up with the image below, which is going to win no Pulitzer Prize.

No pictures. A story repeated. Completely out of date. Useless. So, it's primitive at the moment. But the AI engines are all getting closer to journalism and are bound to get better. Users can already dial in tone and personality. Elon Musk's Grok has just launched a new 'sexy' mode. Inevitably, AI is converging with porn.

THE DAILY CHRONICLE

SATURDAY, MARCH 29, 2025

EU LEADERS AGREE TO NEW MIGRATION DEAL

European Union leaders have reached an agreement on a new migration deal aimed at sharing responsibility for asylum seekers among member states. The deal includes strictes border-controls, faster asylum procedures, and a more equitatble distribution of migrants across bloc.

TENSIONS RISE IN ISRAELI-PROTEST ERUPT

Large-scale protests have erupted across Israel in response to the ongoing conflict with Palestinian militants. Demonstrators are calling for an end to the violence. and criticizing the government's handling of the situation.

U.S. STRIKES IRAN-LINKED TARGETS IN SYRIA

The United States has conducted airstrikes on Iran linked targets in Syria, in response to recent attacks on U.S. forces in the region. The strikes targeted facilities used by Iranian-backed militias, aming to deter further aggression.

HARRIS MAKES CASE FOR RE-ELECTION BID

Vice President Kamala Harris delivered a speech outlining her accomplishments and vision - for re election alongside President

HARRIS MAKES CASE FOR RE-ELECTION BID

Vice President Kamala Harris delivered a speech outlining ner accomplishments and vision for the future, as she begins to make a case for re-election alongside President Joe Biden.

In the brave new world that's upon us, highly stylistic, funny, opinionated and insightful journalists like Bari Weiss, Julie Burchill,[61] Rod Liddle and Jeremy Clarkson are surely safe for now. None of the AI engines are yet capable of simulating such voices in full flight. They're incapable of style or even of accuracy. I asked ChatGPT to simulate a passage by H.L. Mencken. It produced drivel. Artificial intelligence seems destined to be served to us in several flavours but none of them are yet very tasty. I asked it to tell me what Robert Louis Stevenson thought of Pézenas and it replied with direct quotes from him describing his visit. Except he was never there. Under certain circumstances, ChatGPT proffers pure invention.

25

THE HAND THAT FEEDS...

The result of subsidies is not only economic efficiency but also the perpetuation of vested interests that thrive on government largesse rather than competition and will fight tooth and nail to preserve their privileges, no matter how inevitable or inefficient the system may be.'—Milton Friedman

Following the Walter Shapiro-inspired stricture of my argument (A, B, 3), we come to point B: the media is on welfare. Governments in countries that have represented themselves as democracies and boasted of their commitment to human rights and liberty of expression, have put on the payroll the very journalists who are supposed to be holding them to account. In France, Canada, Germany, Switzerland and beyond, a response to the failings of newspapers has been government intervention, keeping in business papers that would otherwise fail. He who pays the piper calls the tune.

There are many ways to pass taxpayer money to publishers. Until Elon Musk's Department of Government Efficiency put a stop to it, Politico, under the administration of President Joe Biden, the quintessential Washington political platform, received $8 million annually in income from government subscriptions to its so-called Pro service. Pro promises 'unique insights and analysis' from the Politico newsroom. The argument that Politico Pro is different from Politico's news service is nonsense. This was a direct subsidy verging on bribery. Was it mere coincidence that anti-Trump, pro-Biden Politico was the chosen conduit for the notorious letter from 51 former intelligence officials seeking to discredit the *New York Post*'s true Hunter Biden laptop story, for the benefit of then-candidate Joe Biden in 2020?

The US Agency for International Development allocates funds to support 'independent media' outlets abroad, aiming to promote free and unbiased information in developing regions. In the 2025 federal budget, approximately $270 million was designated for such initiatives. Perhaps what's embarrassing here is how cheaply the media can be bought.

The readiness of politicians to subsidise journalism is frequently presented as being in the interests of 'diversity' of opinion but inevitably produces the opposite. It creates a style of journalism that the Belgian-born journalist Florence Aubenas[62] calls the freedom to think and write the same way as everybody else.

Subsidies have thoroughly defanged the French media, which gave President Emmanuel Macron a free ride for years before finally starting to lose faith in Spring 2023 when he disastrously called elections producing a divided National Assembly, a strengthened populist party and an enduring political and economic crisis.

The French government claims its media subsidies guarantee pluralism. But many recipients of state largesse are immensely rich plutocrats. So-called pluralism in practice has mostly defaulted to a smug, narrow, Parisian, groupthink bubble. Real reporting is something the French media has largely abandoned and in the provinces, where local newspaper monopolies stand firm, it's scandalous. I have been reading the *Midi-Libre* newspaper for more than 20 years and have yet to encounter the slightest interest in the conflicted conduct of certain local politicians. The paper is stuffed with government advertising including contract tender offers. All this could be posted online for practically nothing. So a dreadful local paper sails on, paid for by taxpayers.

Those unsubsidised journals and websites that dare to move the permissible limits of discussion ever so slightly are immediately denounced as extremists and a danger to democracy. This is vividly demonstrated by the elite Parisian media attempt to disrupt the unsubsidised CNEWS, owned by government-critic Vincent Bolloré. CNEWS is the leading news station in France and the campaign against it is similar to the campaign in Britain against the disruptive GB News.[63] In a retaliation for the non-conformity of CNEWS, Arcom, the French media regulator, just terminated the frequency allocation to an entertainment TV channel also owned by Bolloré, demonised here as 'France's Murdoch.'

Emmanuel Macron often commandeers the airwaves to share his deep insights. He talked and talked. The regime journalists who were supposed to be questioning him just sat there. It was French journalism at its worst. Not one of the president's assertions was challenged, even his claim that Operation Barkhane, the catastrophic French counter-terrorism operation in Mali, had been 'a success.'

The French Senate reports total public support for the press was €367 million (£319 million) in 2021. That's essentially €1 million (£865,000) a day. Much of it ended up in the pockets of billionaires. The Ministry of Culture says that in 2021, 431 titles received state aid. The newspaper that received the most was the tabloid called *Le Parisien* in Paris and *Aujourd'hui en France* in the provinces: €13,520,000 (£11,730,000). The paper is owned by Bernard Arnault, France's richest man.

Next comes centrist *Le Figaro* owned by Groupe Dassault, the arms manufacturer, with €7.7 million (£6.7 million); *Libération*, the French analog of the *Guardian* with €6.7 million (£5.8 million), and *Le Monde*, the quintessential leftist establishment paper, €5.9 million (£5.1 million). The communist party paper *L'Humanité*, which sells 30,000 copies daily, got €5.1 million (£4.4 million)—about €170 (£147) for every devoted comrade-reader.

In addition to payments made to publishers for every paper sold—a charming conceit as the media digitises—the government hands out funds for modernisation and to subsidise physical distribution of newspapers and magazines. Even the *New York Times*, which prints a Paris edition, has had its hand in the cookie jar. It was a pitiful sum, a few hundred thousand euros, but really. Have they no shame?

Not only are the broadcasters and publishers in France showered with other people's money but individual, licensed journalists also nibble at the trough, enjoying a unique *'niche fiscale'* in which a €7,650 (£6,600) slice of their income is entirely untaxed. This might be considered state aid to a failing profession but don't worry because the nifty French have engineered a 'cultural exception' to normal EU rules.

Canada is marching down the same road. Canadian press subsidies introduced under former Prime Minister Justin Trudeau include the Canadian Journalism Labour Tax Credit, a tax relief on journalists' salaries, a C$595 million (£331 million) media package over five years announced in 2019 and an online news act requiring tech giants like Google to compensate Canadian news outlets for content. Google simply stopped including Canadian media stories in search results. In 2019, as part of the Canadian government's media bailout, Torstar Corporation, the parent company of the Toronto Star, benefited from payroll rebates of C$13,750 per employee.

Content analysis is a tricky to impossible discipline, as I have tried to explain to various academics I have encountered over the years. It fails to analyse what isn't published. They have nevertheless continued to pursue the fruitless path, relying on analysis of what is published and ignoring what is not. So how do you prove that the subsidised media in Canada and France and elsewhere do or do not refrain from biting the hands that feed them? To me the empirical evidence is clear enough but this is in the eye of the beholder. That the question exists is problem enough. As traditional media continues to struggle, governments continue to pour money down the rathole. Here's a better idea. Let the dying die. It is almost certain to make way for something else. Picking losers and subsidising them seems to be the order of the day. Subsidies in the cause of pluralism achieve the exact opposite.

26

CONTROLLING THE PRESENT

'If liberty means anything at all, it means the right to tell people what they do not want to hear'—George Orwell

One night, I met a Russian journalist at a reception at the Soviet embassy in London, right after the Berlin Wall had collapsed. He was looking for a job. He worked for the Russian news agency TASS and was probably a spy. Nevertheless I asked him whether there was a censor in Russian newsrooms and he replied, 'of course not, we know what we're allowed to write.'

Having considered points A and B, we arrive at point 3: News is what someone doesn't want printed and there seems less and less of it around. News, already threatened by AI, contaminated by invisible subsidies, is under attack from increasing censorship, even in countries that pay lip service to liberty of expression.

I'd thought we were lucky in the west to have escaped Soviet-style censorship or even much self-censorship. America has its First Amendment, Europe its human rights convention guaranteeing the right to receive and impart information. These rights are being trampled. Where there are limits, we are told, it's to protect us from hate and to uphold 'community standards.' Yet communities left to their own devices are often rather good at upholding standards without help from the government. Community notes on X is a rapid and effective riposte to deliberate misinformation. A new golden age of censorship nevertheless beckons, the censors armed with tools unimaginable to the *index librorum prohibitorum*, the compilers of the list of the Vatican's banned books.

Both media and individuals are kept in line. A censorship complex involves governments, foundations, media companies and now the burgeoning misinformation and disinformation industries. The Center for Countering Digital Hate, a British not-for-profit, non-governmental organisation, is funded by philanthropic trusts and public donations. Its former director is now chief of staff to Keir Starmer. Amongst its stated aims is the suppression of X. And since the Charlie Hebdo massacre in Paris in which 12 people were killed by Islamic gunmen, there is one topic that can be approached only with the utmost caution.

Across Europe, governments are relentlessly attacking social media platforms for alleged disinformation and hate posted by users. Britain's Ofcom has demanded the right to censor the American social media platform Gab, even though it has no legal presence in Britain. The Digital Services Act is an EU regulation aimed at creating a 'safer digital space' by holding online platforms accountable for illegal and harmful content. Safer for whom? It is a charter for outsourcing censorship to social media platforms who risk fines of up to 6% of their global annual turnover for failure to remove 'harmful' content. Harmful to whom? There is a broad ambition within the EU to become the global regulator of digital content. The DSA empowers the EU to enforce compliance with European standards worldwide. Germany has been especially aggressive arresting those suspected of improper posting. The victim of a sexual assault recently received a heavier sentence than her attacker, after she identified him on social media.

In *Unherd* in February 2025, Wolfgang Munchau, the director of the Eurointelligence consultancy, wrote: 'What sustains the EU is not a democratic mandate, but the mainstream media, academia, and think tanks—a blob of organisations that together exert indirect control over what gets discussed and published. You will not find editorials in German newspapers in support of the Alternative for Germany (AfD), despite the fact that this party now accounts for approximately 20% of popular support. The new Right-wing parties communicate through social media instead. This is why the EU is so focused on content moderation for social media, and it's why we have seen a recent explosion of fact-checking units in broadcasting companies and media organisations.'

But the Left is rarely subjected to such fact-checking. Quite a few members of the blob have abandoned X for the alternative Bluesky, which resembles the old Twitter. There, on a much smaller scale, the old echo chamber still works. There, users describe the Trump presidency as a *coup d'état*, and still think that Ukraine is winning the war. No one interrupts them—or checks any facts.

The EU's decision to ban Russian state-controlled media outlets, such as RT and Sputnik, was an unequivocal demonstration of its readiness to suppress voices it deems harmful or contradictory to its narratives. These actions, justified on the grounds of combating disinformation and protecting public order, set a concerning precedent for the future of free speech in Europe. If the EU can justify banning media outlets from non-member countries, what is to stop it from censoring domestic voices that dissent from the majority view or criticise governmental policies?

Britain is leading the way, unfortunately. It has criminalised out of bounds social media postings. We digital pioneers, way back when, thought the internet would route around censorship. How naive we were. Government has found effective tools to suppress free speech and legally harass and punish those dissenting from approved narratives.

AI has made censorship even easier, if crude. No platform wants to risk enormous fines for not censoring enough, so many censor even innocuous material using AI solutions designed to help organisations ensure the legal compliance of online posts: weapons of mass deletion. These tools monitor, filter and manage content to adhere to legal standards and community guidelines. They're on sale now: Tremau software 'centralises and optimises Trust & Safety processes, 'ensuring compliance with regulations like the Digital Services Act; Checkstep is an AI-driven moderation platform capable of scanning text, images, and videos, to detect and manage harmful material; Bloomfire's moderation tools allow for editing, approving, or archiving submissions, and is optimised for the office, to ensure employees tow the line in their electronic communications. Big Brother is watching.

In the UK the government uses hate speech legislation as a primary tool to suppress unacceptable narratives. Home Secretary Yvette Cooper has promised a strengthened commitment to clamping down on 'harmful' beliefs in a broad-reaching so-called Online Safety Bill. This is essentially a blasphemy law criminalising negative opinions about Islam. But the lights have been going out for some time. As of December 2024, police forces in England and Wales had recorded over 133,000 so-called non-crime hate incidents[64] since their introduction in 2014, averaging approximately 13,000 per year. There's no clear metric showing how many of these are related to social media posts but likely most are. Lucy Connolly, the wife of a Conservative councillor, recently received a 31-month prison sentence for inciting racial hatred after calling for the burning of hotels housing asylum seekers.

The Metropolitan Police Service arrested and charged 5332 individuals for committing crimes under the Communications Act 2003, for offenses such as sending offensive or menacing messages via public electronic communication networks.

In July 2024, a horrific attack in Southport, Merseyside resulted in the deaths of three young girls during a Taylor Swift-themed dance class. The attacker, Axel Rudakubana (17), was arrested and later pleaded guilty to the murders. Hundreds were arrested and many jailed for social media posts while the police dissembled with fake news that the attacker was Welsh. In fact, he was the Welsh-born child of a Rwandan asylum seeker accused of war crimes. The government said there was no evidence of a link to terrorism. Rudakubana was manufacturing ricin in his basement.

The media has been largely indifferent to the march of censors and only paid attention when one of our own, *Daily Telegraph* columnist Alison Pearson, was visited by Essex police over a hurty X post.

The case was dropped after an uproar. But cumulatively the message is clear. Offend certain people, expect a visit from the police.

Undoubtedly there is much vile speech on social media, many ghastly people exploiting it for vicious purposes, but the tools being used are so blunt that perfectly legitimate comment is suppressed.

I was myself suspended from X after the October 7 Hamas attack when an irony-deficient algorithm determined that I had called for the ethnic cleansing of Jews from Israel. In fact, I'd posted a map illustrating the ethnic cleansing of Jews from across the middle east, showing Israel as the only country in which it was safe to be a Jew. I captioned it, 'Israel Next.' This was deemed hate speech. Algorithms don't do irony. My appeals were ignored. So, apparently, even I have been guilty of hate speech.

I was a collateral victim. Little now posted escapes a filter. The former administration in America and governments in Europe have routinely 'engaged' with social media companies to manage the dissemination of information. In August 2024, the Biden administration 'requested' that Facebook censor certain COVID-19-related posts, including memes and satirical content, which it deemed misinformation. In February 2024, it was revealed that the Biden administration was exploring the development of artificial intelligence tools aimed at identifying and managing misinformation online. Unless the tide is turned, such tools will lead to increased censorship as only governments decide what is true.

In October 2020, the *New York Post* published a story alleging that Hunter Biden, son of then-presidential candidate Joe Biden, had introduced a Ukrainian businessman to his father. The story was based on emails purportedly retrieved from a laptop belonging to Hunter Biden. The laptop was denounced as characteristic of Russian disinformation by 51 former intelligence officers. The media and tech bros immediately kowtowed. Social media platforms, notably Twitter and Facebook, took steps to limit the spread of this article, citing concerns over the origins of the material. Twitter, now X, temporarily blocked users from sharing the link and locked the New York *Post*'s account.

In a speech to the Munich Security Conference in February, 2025, Vice President JD Vance warned, 'in Britain and across Europe, free speech, I fear, is in retreat.'

'The threat that I worry the most about vis à vis Europe is not Russia, it's not China, it's not any other external actor. And what I worry about is the threat from within. The retreat of Europe from some of its most fundamental values, values shared with the United States of America.'

He added: 'Dismissing people, dismissing their concerns ... shutting down media, shutting down elections... protects nothing. It is the most surefire way to destroy democracy ... If you're running in fear of your own voters, there is nothing America can do for you.'

Keir Starmer did not attend. The audience sat in silence. The BBC security correspondent called the speech 'weird.' The point Vance was making was that the United States would no longer defend Europe, if Europe was going to abandon shared democratic values including freedom of speech. A point wilfully ignored by many European commentators.

The media in Britain is becoming curiously detached from the battle against the censors, probably because the targets of the censors have so far been the social media networks that the mainstream media consider competition. But if first they come for the bloggers, who will they come for next? Witch hunters are always hunting for new witches.

I ran into Piers Morgan at Royal Ascot. They let practically anyone into the Royal Enclosure these days—him, me. I told him the story of my dog Bella, recently cancelled by her GPS tracking company after I petulantly declined its offer of a rainbow Pride tracker. He loved it and had Bella and me on his show—the cancelled dog episode still available all over YouTube, and it generated about 40,000 comments. Bella was the hero of the Woke resistance. An incidental affirmation of the ancient journalism maxim that dog stories still pile them in.

Morgan is writing a book, *Woke Is Dead: How Common Sense*

Triumphed in an Age of Total Madness, set to be published by Harper NonFiction in October 2025. Morgan explores the global rejection of Woke ideology, addressing topics such as the gender divide and the erosion of free speech. He argues that the rise of Woke culture led to increased division and confusion, and he advocates for a return to common sense in a post-woke society. I disagree that Woke is dead. Piers is wrong. Everything moves in cycles and the recent vibe shift caused by the election of Donald Trump has put the Woke on the defensive, after years of uncontested progress. But they've not gone away. Newspapers that profess to be anti-Woke still kowtow to the pronoun ideologues. Describing a sexual assault by a male claiming to be a woman, The *Daily Mail* unapologetically referred to 'her penis.'

27

THE END OF THE NEWS MACHINE?

'Citizen journalism is the future. It's by the people, for the people.'
—*Elon Musk*

And so to point 3, after which I shall retire to my garden. Literally, because as soon as I hit the send button dispatching this tale to the publisher, I am off to Jardiland. Voltaire, arguably among the greatest troublemaking journalists, called his satirical masterpiece *Candide, On Optimism.* It's my Desert Island book. Voltaire is a fine role model. By optimism Voltaire really meant pessimism but he was a canny enough provocateur to know that few want to read a book that is wholly miserable. So he concludes with a redemption of sorts, ultimately sparing his protagonist from the horrors of war, natural disaster, enslavement and betrayal, to let him dig potatoes.

I try to be my normal cheerful self, but as far as the news goes, it's hard to be optimistic. Our industry looks like Voltaire's Lisbon, after the earthquake. The readers don't believe us. The governments subsidise and censor us. Physical newspapers are missed only as bird cage liners. I haven't bought one in years, except occasionally the *Daily Mail,* when I have written something for them, for nostalgia's sake. The British police are arresting people for hurty posts on Facebook. American colleagues are throwing tantrums as their world disintegrates. Journalists on TV are being paid by the government. Social and workplace platforms are systematically monitored by robots. Artificial Intelligence is coming to rip our guts out. I used to be a great advocate of listening to the engineers. It's too late for that. The engineers have taken over. The future of media is going to be defined by code, not journalists.

If we're all journalists, *pace* Elon Musk, where is the news? In 1988 I was on C-Span, the American public affairs network, with Maggie Brown of the then-new *Independent*. (The newspaper was to survive 30 years, before abandoning paper to chance its fortunes on the internet. Its independence is guaranteed by the Russian oligarch Alexander Lebedev, a former KGB officer, who bought the title in 2010.)

Our job was to explain the British press to Americans. Total daily newspaper sales in Britain were then colossal, 18 million a day. Today the figures are so embarrassing they're no longer published, but are perhaps 2-4 million.

The first-ever tweet was posted by Jack Dorsey, co-founder of Twitter, on March 21, 2006, which is as good a day as any to proclaim that the new world. began. It read: 'just setting up my twttr'. He typed this not in any newsroom but in the tech hub of South Park, San Francisco. His tweet wasn't profound, indeed it was resonant of the first banal words spoken over the telephone in 1876 by Alexander Graham Bell to his assistant, 'Mr Watson come here. I want to see you.' Engineers aren't poets.

Yet that day symbolically marked the beginning of the end of the news as we knew it. Because henceforth, journalists were no longer competing just against each other, but against everyone. Welcome to the globalised press club. Elon Musk is not entirely wrong that we are all journalists now. Anyone can speak unto nations, from their mobile phone. Although some of these new journalists are better than others.

Like Schrödinger's cat, news and journalism are simultaneously alive and dead. It's in what physicists call a quantum superposition. There are sparkling journalists to be found, some of them having emerged from the ether of YouTube and X. There are many start-ups and initiatives to rekindle journalism. But many hallowed institutions of journalism look like a train wreck. There's no longer an evening newspaper in London.

A handful of legacy media seems to have successfully traversed the slough of despond, although leaving much of their credibility behind. Notably the *New York Times,* now more aptly characterised as the *New Woke Times,* with more than $1 billion in digital revenue and more than 10 million digital subscribers. I subscribe, but mainly for Wordle. But its daily print circulation has collapsed from 1.1 million in 1988 to under 300,000 now. Its famous motto, 'All the news that's fit to print,' has become, essentially, all the news we think you should be told.

Others are slow horses, like the *Washington Post,* glorious for its role in the Watergate story, now the plaything of Amazon tycoon Jeff Bezos, who has proven clueless as a proprietor. The paper is losing close to $100 million a year and has given up much pretence of unbiased journalism. Local newspapers everywhere are on their knees. Gannett's New Jersey paper the *Record* has lost 90 per cent of its circulation since 2013.

As newspapers move online, they are no longer really newspapers but participants in a cornucopia of clickbait, driving reader-engagement metrics. True, the headlines of yesteryear[65] can be considered a form of bait, especially the front-page splash headlines that sold the newspaper at news stands. But newspaper headlines were pushing news, not cat videos. The paper as a whole was coherent. A product put together by professional news journalists has dematerialised into an incoherent mess of hyperlinks. It's degenerated into informational junk food, empty digital calories. The so-called online newspaper is barely a newspaper. The mastheads have been appropriated for a product that's quite different, publishing material with little relationship to news. And even remaining print newspapers have degenerated, as they survive by feeding off the digital environment. Journalists sit at their desk and plunder X for their stories. It's a snake eating its own tail. Nobody in the click-bait mills has ever pushed the send button yelling, 'wonderful story,' like the deputy city editor of the *Detroit Free Press.* Instead the suits in the C-suite measure engagement.

As squirming media companies engage in their financial ballet-ics, there have emerged new knights errant, individual journalists who are striking out on their own, with some success. Many are using a platform called Substack, that allows writers to publish and monetise through paid subscriptions. Launched in 2017, it provides an oven-ready solution for independent journalists, analysts, and creators to reach audiences directly. The platform takes 10% of the gross revenue. These are not really digital newspapers because they rarely cover news: they are digital viewspapers, composed of com-mentary and strong opinions.

While platforms like Substack make this feasible, to present a viable media product to cut through all the noise takes a lot of talent and effort. Journalists are not inherently skilled at the technical tasks required but are learning. The poster child for building Substack into a viable news business is the celebrated Bari Weiss, who has converted her snarky sense of humour into something looking like a viable business.

In January 2021, she left the *New York Times* after awful rows to start the *Free Press*. Her *Free Press* bears no relation to the *Detroit Free Press* newspaper, which I have discussed elsewhere. But the title offers a similar attitude.

The Bari *Free Press* by January 2025 had 136,000 subscribers paying $8 a month each, generating an annual revenue of around $13 million. The *New York Times* wasn't paying her that much.

The *Free Press* went out of its way to be fair to Trump and his voters hence emerged from the 2024 presidential election not humiliated and embarrassed, like MSNBC, ABC's The Voice, the *Washington Post*, and the many others that covered up for Biden's infirmity and relentlessly attacked Trump. They doubtless felt virtu-ous, but should have known better.

Others abandoning corporate media include the writer-broad-caster Piers Morgan. In January 2025, Morgan acquired full owner-ship of his YouTube-based show, Piers Morgan Uncensored, from Murdoch's News UK through his production company, Wake Up Productions. He has momentum: nine million followers on X. His program is getting between 1-3 million views. Tucker Carlson, fired from Fox News, launched the Tucker Carlson Network (TCN), and has around 500,000 regular viewers. It used to cost a fortune to establish a television news network. Now, the cost of entry is approaching zero for the most basic broadcaster speaking unto nation from his sitting room. But producing viewable television demands talent.

Podcasts have been a surprise in the great replacement of the mainstream. Radio was pushed aside by television but its progeny the podcast is now reviving the spoken word. Podcaster Joe Rogan beats Piers Morgan, Tucker Carlson and the *New York Times* for reach, with 20m followers across numerous platforms. Trump did Rogan and won the election. Kamala Harris declined. Although primarily a revival of voice, podcasts are often available in a video talking heads format on YouTube and streaming platforms.

In the 1930s and 1940s, radio commentators like Edward R. Murrow and Walter Winchell reached 10-20 million listeners per broadcast. These audiences are back. Mr and Mrs America, all the ships at sea, and much of the rest of the world, is listening to podcasts.

A thousand more flowers are blooming, and as many are withering. Some creators are just happy to share their thinking, without much expectation of profit. There's also the phenomenon of the 'influencer' which I'm reluctant to call journalism although it sometimes crosses the line. Clothes, cars, fitness, food—there are influencers for all of these and a thousand more categories and if it's not exactly journalism, it's competition for screen time, and another challenge to the journalists who had imagined it was territory of their own. Is a plus-size influencer getting a million views on TikTok for her ranting against too-small airline seats a journalist? Elon Musk would say so.

Early digital pioneers are being challenged to keep up. How quickly the innovators have fallen. Among the witherers in the new media order is the Huffpost online news site launched in 2005 by Arianna Huffington, and proudly progressive, entirely digital. It expanded, was bought out. It found itself on the wrong side of the vibe shift after the victory of Donald Trump. In January 2025 it laid off a fifth of its staff. In February, Trump ridiculed one of its reporters in a huddle on Air Force One. The supposedly achingly-hip Vice, in which Murdoch was an investor, and once valued at billions of dollars, is now bankrupt.

The highly personal newsletter has made a comeback, offering journalism reminiscent of that of the legendary I.F. Stone.[66] Andrew Sullivan, a former editor of the *New Republic* and columnist for the *Sunday Times*, walked away from newspapers and magazines to found his own politics Substack, The *Daily Dish*. Five years later he has 20,000 subscribers paying $50 each. It's a million dollar business and with no numpties in the C-suite, because the C-suite is Sullivan's kitchen.

There's evidence of a new eco-system developing of creative clusters breaking through to million-dollar revenues but is this enough, and will outstandingly successful entrants be picked off by media companies and private equity? Efforts at digital local news are praiseworthy but of variable quality and viability. None has close to the influence that local newspapers once had. Merrill Brown, who now runs a group of edgy news blogs and who was one of the first to warn of the decline of print, is enthusiastic for the many new models starting to appear, including foundation funding.

'Little of this existed a decade ago. Is it all working? No, especially in the context of actually building workable revenue models. But there's an infrastructure and hundreds of news products that are thriving editorially and providing public service,' he tells me.

'While the *Washington Post* and Los Angeles *Times* suffer with their bumbling billionaires, the Boston Globe and Minneapolis Star *Tribune* are doing fairly well with theirs. The Philadelphia Inquirer is doing OK with its billionaire-funded foundation organisation.'

These seem like shaky foundations to me. It's a complicated, nuanced and rapidly evolving market. Now, into this Capernaum, has arrived Elon Musk, with journalism pretentions of his own.

He's integrating AI with X and thinks of X as a media platform, not a social network. Musk has 212 million followers on X, and a greater media reach than possibly anyone else on the planet. Is he now a journalist, too? Yes, by his own definition. Will he be the new Citizen Kane? He's already eclipsed Rupert Murdoch. 'Citizen journalism is the future. It's by the people, for the people,' he says. While the strict accuracy of some of his X pronouncements is disputed, alleged inexactitude has never been a disqualification from journalism.

So we're all journalists but news is dead. The news is inaudible amidst the clamour. It's hard to believe anything and likely to get harder as artificial intelligence tells us what's important to note.

I'm cynical but expect many of those running news businesses will be blindsided again. It's another perfect storm, like the internet. The tanks of the tech bros are parked on the media company lawns. Robojournalism is landing.

Newspapers are already items for museums.[67] And a museum is where news is going.

When I was in Washington and witnessed the explosion in telecommunications, and how quickly the networks were saturated and there were demands for more data speed, more storage, more bandwidth, I developed a theory that there was no limit to the amount of information that humans wish to communicate with one another. This is another of my Rules of Journalism.

But where in this cacophony is the news? Perhaps we're now all journalists but neither are all journalists equal. And little of the colossal amount of content created resembles what we used to take for news. Sure, plenty of views. Lots of choices of elite Substacks. Plenty of cat clips.

Amidst this new crisis for journalism, smart, elite journalists— true to form—are missing the story, guarding their *amour propre* and ignoring the oncoming steamroller. Axios CEO Jim VandeHei staged a melt down at The National Press Club in Washington in 2024 after Elon Musk announced, 'You Are The Media Now,' declaring that everyone was now a journalist. In a speech characterised by some present as a hysterical rant, he insisted that only the traditional media could claim that status. Memo to Mr. VandeHei: those gates have been torn down and gatekeepers like him are no longer special and no longer trusted. He might imagine that with his website he is the future of news. He can hissy-fit all he wants. But what's he defending? Call it the mainstream media, corporate media, establishment media, whatever you want. It's on its knees.

Is VandeHei suggesting that Axios is the future? Founded by himself and two colleagues who broke away from Politico, itself a quintessentially establishment medium, that now turns out to have been lavishly government subsidised. They then sold out to Cox Enterprises for $525 million. Yup, he's a man of the people, with his impeccable credentials as a millionaire Democrat.

Are we supposed to believe BBC Verify, whose star journalist Marianna Spring faked her resume to get her job? The consumers of information will decide for themselves but may be unlikely to conclude that Spring's pronouncements or Rachel Maddow literally breaking down crying on live television because she's upset by Donald Trump represent anything more than performance. Maddow is the "beating heart" of MSNBC, says my friend Eugene Robinson, a contributor to the network, tells me. Very well, but the network owned by Comcast has lost half its audience since Trump's election in November 2024.

The news is changing in innumerable ways. News as we knew it, reasonably credible, at least enjoying the confidence of its readers, curated by people with authority and experience, news that some people don't want printed, popular news for ordinary folk, that news is dead. If extraordinary efforts are made, some picture of the world as it is can be assembled. But few have the time or inclination. There is no limit to the amount of information that humans seek to communicate amongst ourselves, and never has it been so easy to share it. But the consequence is that we're drowning in content and never have we understood so little about what is going on.

28

ADVICE TO TROUBLEMAKERS

'If your mother says she loves you, check it out.'—Slogan on the wall of the fabled Chicago City News Bureau.

And so I come to the end of my story, the Shock of the News. It's really the story of how I was always naughty, yet managed to find an occupation where this was an advantage. It was another era. I'm not sure I'd get away with it if starting now.

Let me tell you about some of the people who made the journey possible, starting with Mrs Miller, my tolerant wife of more than 51 years at the time of writing. She has been a horrified witness to many of the events and exploits I have described. She's a working class hero in her own right, and certainly the only graduate of Immaculata High School in Detroit to have been awarded a CBE by King Charles.

Tolerance is a virtue in the spouse of a journalist, especially one with their own career. We've established a firewall. I stay well away from her business, and she only interferes a little with mine, rolling her eyes when I am being boring.

After we met we quickly discovered that as children, separated by an ocean, we had both read Swallows and Amazons by Arthur Ransome. Ransome was a bold journalist and a great writer of fiction for children. As a journalist for the *Manchester Guardian* he interviewed Lenin and chided him for insufficient revolutionary zeal. He later married Trotsky's secretary. But Swallows and

Amazons is why he is remembered. Mrs Miller is like the Swallow Susan Walker in the book, responsible and sensible. I am often neither. I'm much more like a male version of the Amazon Nancy Blackett, setting off fireworks, defying authority. Mrs M was a journalist herself before going over to the dark side of the law. She still laughs at my jokes, however, and tolerates my irritating tendency to say, 'I told you so'. Her efforts to improve me have been relentless if not successful. She is a fierce competitor in Scrabble. She was taught how to spell by nuns.

Who else helped me write this book are those who fed me with stories for life. If we are all what we eat, writers are also who they read. I have met many extraordinary people in my peregrinations but journalists and writers have nourished me as no politician or celebrity ever has.

I point as an example to the late Brenda Maddox, a daughter of Quincy, Massachusetts, futurist, literary biographer and *Economist* journalist. She occupies a prominent position in my Pantheon of colleagues, mentors, role models and inspirations. Next to her imagined marble bust in my hall of fame is that of her husband, the late Sir John Maddox, the editor of Nature, who was never wrong about anything.

In 1972, Brenda wrote the book *Beyond Babel*[68] predicting the media and communications revolution that subsequently occurred. Her book was little noticed at the time but thrilling to me. She predicted that if a coaxial cable were threaded throughout American cities and fashioned into a national network, it could deliver letters, library books and act as a computer terminal. She had, in fact, anticipated the Internet, if not in detail, then in principle.

Brenda was a serious journalist but had a golden rule to get as many jokes, double-entendres and witty literary references as possible into every story. It was a technique that built on the Harry Evans[69] dictum to take light subjects seriously and serious subjects lightly. I worked with her when she was at the *Economist* and in Washington. Even shopping for shoes with her was an adventure. Everything she said was clever and I wished I'd said it. Her biographies of Nora Barnacle, the wife of James Joyce, and Rosalind Franklin, one of the pioneers of the science of DNA, are astonishing for their revelation and insight. She taught me to always *cherchez la femme*.

John was a chemist and physicist who was editor of the world's most important science journal *Nature* for 22 years. He smoked like a steam-engine driver, which eventually killed him. Fiercely Welsh, he had a debenture at Cardiff Arms Park. I remember lunch at an Italian place in Kensington where he told me that his proprietors, the Macmillan[70] family, were so posh that they referred to their editors as servants. We discussed science and energy at the Maddox farm house in Wales, in a valley so infested with BBC executives that Brenda called it Media Gulch. He wasn't contrarian, merely rigorous. John maintained that there was no energy crisis, at a time when we were supposedly running out of fuel. More oil remained to be discovered than had been consumed, he said.

Anthropogenic global warming was an unproven scientific theory, he said. Which seems to be the case, still. Which was no reason not to be respectful to the environment, he added. He liked a tidy farmer. He would have laughed at Net Zero and its cod maths and shaken his head in disbelief at the elite kowtow to Greta Thunberg. He was working on a book about what remains to be discovered. Plenty, it turned out.[71] Developing a vaccine against AIDS would take 10 years at least, or maybe longer, he predicted. He was right. We're still waiting. It's a shame we didn't have his wisdom during Covid-19 when media and political hysteria overwhelmed rationality.

At the *Sunday Times* I was surrounded by many legends of Fleet Street, although they were dinosaurs really. They'd been the Biggest Beasts in the jungle and the jungle was going or gone and their extinction was imminent. These were not guys who were grasping the Internet. They knew a lot about journalism, however.

The greatest of all the ink-in-the-veins newspaper men I have known was Tony Bambridge, the managing editor of the *Sunday Times* in the Andrew Neil era, cruelly taken from us by cancer in

1997. Bambridge was a master of newsroom intrigue. He had sharp antennae for a dodgy story and could detect an inventive expense account by smell. When Sue Douglas tried to poach AA Gill from the *Sunday Times* to join the *Sunday Express*, Gill was trying to wring out more money when Bambridge stood up, extended his hand and said, 'Congratulations, Adrian, you are now the television critic of the *Sunday Express*.' Gill stayed put.

Roy Greenslade was another brilliant journalist at the *Sunday Times*. In 2021 Greenslade finally revealed in an article for the *British Journalism Review* that he had supported the IRA since the early 1970s. He had written for the Sinn Féin newspaper *An Phoblacht* under a pseudonym in the late 1980s.

Yet he presided genially over the 'shallow end' of the Wapping warehouses where the *Sunday Times* and *Times* had decanted. The new liberation from the unions meant we could print bigger papers. The lifestyle pieces produced down at the Greenslade end were crucial to what was becoming a rocketing circulation. Ironically, Greenslade the lefty was also Greenslade the Wapping scab. Yet he was never punished by his leftist friends for this, and went on to be a columnist for the *Guardian* and a professor of journalism. Perhaps he was spying on us for the Provos. I can't imagine why they'd bother.

Greenslade brought a relaxed competence to wrangling the diverse talents he overlooked. Nigella Lawson was doing the Look pages with Sara Miller, who went on to Condé Nast while Nigella charmed and conquered the world. Helen Fielding was cooking up Bridget Jones. Jane Thynne, now an admired novelist, was writing features. My tiny Screen and Print department, with me and Alex Sutherland, was part of this merry 'shallow end' tribe, isolated from the 'deep end' of the news and business desks at the other end of the building. Greenslade was funny, avuncular, amusing and unflappable. How were we to know he was IRA-adjacent? My memory of him is that he was a talented journalist.

Maurice Chittenden who was de facto chief reporter and night desk wizard was the cagiest of veterans at the *Sunday Times*. His book *Exclusive, the Last Days of Fleet Street—My Part in its Downfall,* is a classic memoir of a vanishing breed. Chittenden had the finest contact book in Fleet Street, thicker than one of the old telephone directories. He was capable of putting together a front-page splash in minutes.

Many others have inspired me. Michael Kinsley at the *New Republic* was the first to publish my freelance work after I moved to Washington in 1980. He's *hors de combat* now with Parkinson's Disease but still the most brilliant guy in the room, says a friend who saw him recently. Jim Dewey at the *Detroit Free Press* taught me to ask more questions. Marie Colvin, whom I last saw in the Bar America in Kukes, Albania, and who was killed in Homs, Syria in 2012, was the bravest journalist I ever met.

Kelvin MacKenzie was editor of the *Sun* from 1981-1994 when the paper sold more than four million copies a day. His journalism was a master class in mischief-making. He gave the English language an unforgettable phrase. He said the purpose of the paper was to put a ferret up the trousers of politicians. When the paper's stance had to change abruptly, he would famously shout out to the newsroom, 'reverse ferret.' The expression has entered the language as a metaphor for an abrupt reversal, having been used by the *New York Times* and former British prime minister Boris Johnson.

When Kelvin fired the paper's astrologer, he supposedly asked him, 'I suppose you know why you're here?' 'No.' 'That you don't know proves how useless you are. Because you're fired.'

Forward-thinking journalists are surprisingly rare and crop up in odd places. Arnold Rosenfeld, the managing editor of the *Dayton Daily News*, was the first to tell me, in 1975, that newspapers would be personalised, every copy different, tuned to the interests and needs of the reader. This newspaper he imagined, although it will be in digital form and not on paper, is finally about to happen, thanks to AI. Although I suppose the reader can print it out, if they wish, making Arnold 100% right. Anyway, he was a brilliant editor. He let me run with stories and didn't care where they led.

Al Warren, the crusty veteran who spent the Second World War hunched over radio sets, who took the bet on launching *Communications Daily*, and demanded live television on airplanes when it was considered impossible, was another look-ahead journalist. He also taught me the value of an afternoon nap and a large tip to the Maitre d' at the celebrated Washington Palm restaurant.

Sarah Baxter who edited my column at the *Sunday Times* is a clever journalist, despite the handicap of having attended Oxford University. She created a column called Enemy of the People which was a faux-Stalinist denunciation of some unfortunate in the news. The lawyers eventually shut it down. She's gone back to America and is running the memorial Marie Colvin Center for International Reporting at Stony Brook University. She's another troublemaker, but perhaps she doesn't get as close to the line.

Rolfe Tessem, yet another of my cohort at the *Michigan Daily*, taught me how to see. It's amazing how many journalists don't look at what is in front of them, their noses down in the handouts. He was a brilliant photographer and journalist who knew how words and pictures work together on a newspaper page. He was also extraordinarily adept technically, and a big thinker, and the first person to tell me to look into the thing called the internet. After university he went straight to Washington as a cameraman for ABC News, which was introducing the first video cameras. He went on to be executive producer of Nick News, with his partner the fine misbehaving Texas journalist Linda Ellerbee, who is too like me for us to get along. Of course subsequently, just as we are all journalists now *pace* Musk, we are also now all photographers and videographers, using the phone already in our pocket. Another skill of yesterday has gone. Rolfe is a ham radio operator hence hardcore geek. He is also a superb aerobatic pilot. I know this because I am alive. I was his passenger on an exciting series of death-defying manoeuvres over Cape Cod, and lived to tell the tale. Before getting into his Decathlon, a powerful, gaily painted single engine aerobatic airplane with a high wing, he handed me a parachute. I explained that I did not normally engage in activities requiring a parachute. 'Don't worry about it. It's an FAA regulation. If we crash you'd not get out anyway.' He's retired now and sold the Decathlon but is most likely to be found in the sky in his classic V-tail Beechcraft Bonanza.

Anne-Élisabeth Moutet is a rare non-group-thinking French journalist who lives in Paris and is a member of my secretive and very non-PC WhatsApp group. She is a mistress of aphorism and a renowned hostess attracting *le tout* Paris to her salon, shared with a cat privy to many confidences. She is included in the hall of fame because she writes as sweetly in English as in French, often appearing in English in the *Telegraph* and explaining the English to the French on the news channels here. In addition to my own rules of journalism, see above, she is a lawgiver. 'Never tell your readers your deepest secrets. They don't pay enough,' she says. I have frequently ignored this advice, to my regret.

And then there's Andrew Neil. He has been the animator of many of my adventures in journalism, especially my transition from Washington to London. He's formidable, quick and clever, has the Glaswegian predilection for a punch-up but much gentler in person than his public persona suggests. Michael Portillo, the broadcaster and former Conservative politician, who knows him well, rented the house next door one recent summer and we shared a glass or two of Mas Gabriel and discussed Andrew, fondly. Portillo agreed with me when I advanced the theory that deep down, Andrew's a pussycat, cuddly with claws. The two of them made some great programs together, with Diane Abbot, when she was at her best. Like many great editors he has a phenomenal memory and takes copious notes in a daybook. He has a finely-tuned bullshit detector—although not infallible. He got carried away during Covid, taking an uncharacteristically authoritarian stand against those disputing official narratives about vaccines, lockdowns and masks. We all make mistakes.

Andrew is very savvy on politics and economics in America and France as well as Britain. He was razor-sharp on technology before geek was cool. He understood the Beyond Babel idea of universal connectivity long before it was fashionable.

We've had lots of adventures together. We were in Paris, trying to go to Luxembourg. Andrew I suspected was engaged in some kind of *liaison dangereuse* and I had flown in from London and met him at Charles de Gaulle airport for a connection to Findel airport, the aptly named LUX. Our super-secret mission was a dinner I had organised with the prime minister. We were going to ask him if it was okay, if Sky was thrown out of Britain, if we could set up shop there. But Luxair cancelled its flight. So we chartered a Beechcraft King Air at Le Bourget. Dinner was saved. Andrew insisted that the astronomic cost go on my credit card, not his, as my expenses could be signed by him, whereas his own had to be approved by Rupert Murdoch himself. The prime minister did say, just to complete the tale, that we would be very welcome in the Grand Duchy, so it was mission accomplished.

AFTER THE BINGE

My Lunch with Rupert

How did my job interview on the Fox Lot in Los Angeles go, when Rupert gave me lunch at the Commissary? It was a slightly heady atmosphere. I was fairly intimidated. I tried to advance my theories, but I was missing. He didn't seem that interested. Perhaps his instincts had reached their limits, perhaps I was babbling. He should probably have put me in charge of the internet at News Corporation, if only because at least I had an interest in technology, and had a team up and running, although in retrospect it would probably have ruined my life.

I don't know the Rosebud of Rupert Murdoch—to make a final comparison with Kane—what makes him tick? Was there a lost binky? How to characterise him in a word? A gambler above all, who ended a long winning streak with some bad bets. He was a king, he knew it, and he behaved that way. His impulsiveness was to lead to spectacular failures. In November 1990, facing the inability to meet upcoming loan repayments, Murdoch convened a meeting with 146 global bankers in Sydney to negotiate a standstill agreement, freezing over $8 billion in loans for three years. I wrote a speech for him afterwards, and tried to deal with this humiliation in a passage emphasising the power of resilience. Murdoch angrily scratched it out. 'I'm not reminding them that I went broke,' he snapped

Since I worked for him, he divorced Anna. They were married for 32 years. Her moderating influence stopped Murdoch from running completely amok. Six years after my night on his magic mountain, he abandoned her, to run off with Wendy Deng, an executive in Hong Kong who was leading his push into China. A push that ultimately failed. And as one marriage segued to another, his grand creation, News Corporation, would itself begin to run off the rails. Murdoch's influence would be eclipsed by entirely new media he didn't understand. And he is still paying for his matrimonial incontinence. His children with Deng vastly complicate his $1.7 billion divorce settlement with Anna and have made the Murdoch family succession a spectacle. Life imitating art imitating life, a real-life version of the TV series, Succession, which was unconvincingly denied to be based on the Murdoch story. Wendy Deng would not be the last of Murdoch's wives. He had a fling with Mick Jagger's ex, got engaged, broke it off, and married again, divorced again, and married again.

Murdoch was also a great journalist. He knew how to make a newspaper, as the contents of his trash can in Isleworth revealed to me. Rupert will be the last of the great press barons—along he never got a peerage. Quite possibly one of the few journalists who has behaved worse than me. He's made more trouble than anyone I know.

His newspapering skill, however, is no longer much relevant. He was on the phone daily to Donald Trump daily during the president's first term. Not now. Murdoch is in his nineties. A historical figure. His empire is intact but reduced and unlikely to survive his inevitable demise. He's no longer the bad boy. Musk is the new figure of evil. Murdoch's remaining life seems consumed by his succession, and the catastrophic consequences of his dysfunctional family life. His fall marks the end not just of a dynasty but an era. The new barons are digital.

Despite everything that's happened to the press, the news, newspapers, journalism, my advice to young people who have the urge to be journalists, who may have read this book looking for career advice, is not to be discouraged but to go for it. You will need luck, resilience, curiosity, adaptability and cunning to navigate the shocks to come. Don't be scared to make trouble. The next generation of journalists are going to have to navigate deep waters and timidity is not a characteristic of survival. I wouldn't bother with journalism school. Read chemistry or physics, or, if you must, history or classics. Most journalists are scientific ignoramuses, but technology is where change incubates. Learn a language and use it. You must read everything. You learn to write by reading. And to understand journalism, and the danger of the pack, you must read Scoop. Everything in the book is all still true as I discovered at the Bar America in Kukes, Albania. Although I must include a trigger warning, for some might find the novel offensive by contemporary standards. I just reread it for perhaps the tenth time and it's truly the Shock of the News.

Also, read *Tintin*.

Preferably in French.

ENDNOTES

1   Subsequently the USS Maine did explode in Havana harbour, provoking the headline in the Journal: 'Remember the Maine! To hell with Spain!'

2   Newspapers may have faded but the megalomania of media tycoons endures. Elon Musk and X a contemporary example.

3   *The Chief, the Life of Lord Northcliffe, Britain's Greatest Press Baron* by Andrew Roberts, Simon & Schuster, 2022 is the definitive account.

4   Both launched in 1995.

5   Temporary prefabricated housing developed during Second World War. Of surprising durability. A handful are reportedly occupied today.

6   The London Nobody Knows is a 1967 documentary film narrated by actor James Mason. The film explores the hidden, often overlooked corners of the city during the 'Swinging Sixties,' a time when London was widely celebrated for its cultural vibrancy. However, instead of focusing on the glamorous or iconic landmarks, the film delves into the decaying remnants of Victorian London, capturing the city's underbelly and the lives of its marginalised inhabitants.

7   A tour de force, Withnail and I (1987) was directed by Bruce Robinson and set in 1969, starring Richard E. Grant, Paul McGann and Richard Griffiths.

8   ' England swings like a pendulum do, bobbies on bicycles two by two, Westminster Abbey, the tower of Big Ben, the rosy red cheeks of the little children.'

9   In 1969, Sinclair was arrested for distributing marijuana—specifically for giving two joints to an undercover narcotics officer—and was sentenced to 10 years in prison. The harshness of the sentence sparked widespread criticism and galvanized a high-profile protest movement. This culminated in the 'Free John Now Rally' on December 10, 1971, in Ann Arbor, Michigan, which drew 15,000 people and featured performances by John Lennon, Yoko Ono, Stevie Wonder, and others. The rally, along with growing public pressure, led to Sinclair's release three days later when the Michigan Supreme Court declared the state's marijuana laws unconstitutional. This legal victory also contributed to the decriminalization of marijuana in Ann Arbor and inspired the annual Hash Bash, a pro-legalization event still held today, even though marijuana has been legal in Michigan since 2019.

10   Hunter S. Thomson committed suicide in 2005. He was a famous new journalist who covered the campaign for Rolling Stone magazine and later published the book *Fear and Loathing on the Campaign Trail*, Straight Arrow Books, 1973.

11   A *Daily* colleague who read the manuscript of this book wanted more about the sex. Short of creating a chart of who had sex with whom, I am not sure what she wants. Such a chart would be quite the engrenage.

12   In October 1969, The Michigan *Daily* published LaBour's article titled M*cCartney Dead; New Evidence Brought to Light*. It played a pivotal role amplifying the Paul is dead conspiracy theory, which suggested that Paul McCartney had died in a car accident in 1966 and had been secretly replaced by a look-alike.

13   He bought a suit from Bloomingdales, wore it every day of the campaign, and returned it after he lost, demanding and getting a refund for excessive wear.

14   A stringer in newspaper terminology was a freelance contributor, so-called because contributors were once paid by the length of a string laid along the published copy.

15   Horace Greeley (1811-1872) was founder and editor of the *New York Tribune*, where he championed abolition, worker's rights, and westward expansion, famously urging, 'Go West, young man.'

16   *Once in a Great City: A Detroit Story*. Simon & Schuster 2015.

17   The linotype machine called Monotype in Britain was invented in 1884, revolutionized printing by automating

typesetting, casting entire lines of type in metal, and enabling faster, cheaper production of newspapers and books. It was the Atex of its day.

18   Hyper-violent Jewish pre-WWII gang founded by the Bernstein Brothers in Little Jerusalem on Detroit's Lower East Side.

19   For aficionados, a search of YouTube yields several examples.

20   The City Desk on American newspapers is equivalent to the News Desk in Britain, where the City Desk concerns itself with business, economics and finance.

21   In May 1971 the Anchor Bar was the target of a federal raid. Authorities accused owner Leo Derderian and associate Charles 'Chickie' Sherman of operating a gambling operation generating $40,000 daily.

22   Subsequently bought by Gannett, with predictable consequences.

23   Merged into the Constitution-Journal in 1982.

24   Senator Sam Ervin served as a U.S. Senator from North Carolina from 1954 to 1974. He is best known for his role as the chairman of the Senate Watergate Committee during the early 1970s, where he played a key part in investigating the Watergate scandal.

25   Operation Eagle Claw ended with the failure of 3 out of 8 American helicopters and the subsequent crash of another into a transport aircraft resulting in the deaths of eight servicemen. The hostages were released on 20 January 1981 as Ronald Reagan was inaugurated.

26   The TRS-80 was an early laptop microcomputers with a crude word processor and LCD screen introduced by Tandy Corporation and sold through its RadioShack stores in America starting in 1977. It was one of the first affordable personal computers, priced at $599. Many are still functional today.

27   Later made into a film directed by Ken Russell starring Michael Caine.

28   The concept of a space elevator has fascinated scientists, engineers, and science fiction enthusiasts for over a century. It envisions a cable, or tether, stretching from Earth's surface to geostationary orbit, approximately 22,000 miles (35,786 km) above the equator. This structure would allow vehicles, called climbers, to ascend and descend the cable, transporting cargo and potentially humans into space without the need for rockets. The idea was first proposed by Russian scientist Konstantin Tsiolkovsky in 1895, inspired by the Eiffel Tower. However, the concept remains speculative due to significant technological, material, and logistical challenges .

29   Salvador Dali thought the centre of the universe was Perpignan railway station and painted a famously pornographic picture of it.

30   The EU in 2024 required all mobile devices to recharge using the USB3 standard. Just in time for USB4.

31   The EU continues its interventions in technology, in 1984 imposing a standard for mobile device chargers that will inevitably become obsolete.

32   It was announced in 2024 that lossmaking Sky News will move content behind an online paywall in a shift from linear programming as its revenue streams are 'largely stagnant.'

33   Pillars of established media including Granada Television, Pearson PLC and Reed International.

34   The Leading Article, the editorial in which the corporate view of the paper is expressed.

35   Fox News launched in 1996 quickly became dominant in cable news with its opinion-driven format. Ailes ferociously resisted Murdoch's attempts to impose himself on the network but in 2016 amidst sexual harassment allegations Murdoch regained control and Ailes was forced out. He died in 2017 of a heart attack, aged 77.

36   A definitive account appeared in the *New York Times*, February 13, 2025. It states: '… if he fails to consolidate Lachlan's control over the trust before he dies, the future of his companies will be thrown into uncertainty. The other three siblings could topple their brother and reorient the companies' editorial bent. Or they could simply do nothing and let the trust expire. That is set to happen in 2030, at which point everyone would be free to sell their controlling shares to outsiders.' These documents reveal that in a matter of years, the empire that Rupert spent his life building may no longer be controlled by his family.

37   Twins Sir David and Sir Frederick Barclay also owned the *Daily Telegraph, Sunday Telegraph, Spectator,* and the Ritz Hotel in London. Lloyds bank seized control in 2023. The brothers resided in a mock Gothic castle on the private island of Brecqhou in the Channel Islands.

38   A popular joke in Tirana had a little boy asking his father, 'What did we do before we had candles, baba?' 'We had electricity,' was the reply.

39   Microsoft later withdrew because the conflict of interest was eventually too much to ignore, and it all fell into the hands of NBC, which was itself subsumed by Comcast, which would also eventually seize control of Sky Television in the UK. Comcast grew out of American cable television operations that grew fat on the explosion of channels provoked by communications satellites.

40   Sites was a legendary war correspondent and author of *Swimming with Warlords: A Twelve Year Journey Across the Afghan War, In the Hot Zone: One Man, One Year, Twenty Wars,* and *The Things They Cannot Say: Stories Soldiers Won't Tell You About What They've Seen, Done or Failed to Do in War.*

41   Colvin, who was 56 when she died, was played by Rosamund Pike in *A Private War*, a 2018 film, based on her life.

42   Black Lamb and Grey Falcon by Rebecca West is a monumental travelogue and historical analysis of the Balkans in the late 1930s, essential reading for spies and journalists.

43   Famous for his hysterical overestimation of the likely deaths from Mad Cow Disease and Covid 19.

44   Abigail Woods is a prominent scholar in the field of veterinary history, particularly known for her work on the history of foot-and-mouth disease in Britain. Her most notable work related to FMD is *A Manufactured Plague?: The History of Foot and Mouth Disease in Britain* (published in 2004). This book examines how FMD transitioned from being considered a minor ailment to one of the most feared animal diseases in Britain. Woods argues that much of the fear, tragedy, and sorrow associated with FMD were not due to the disease itself but to the legislative and control measures implemented against it. She posits that FMD is a 'manufactured' plague due to human decisions, particularly around policy, economics, and politics, rather than the biological nature of the disease.

45   *France, a Nation on the Verge of a Nervous Breakdown.* Gibson Square, 2015.

46   The entire population of Béziers, the nearest city to me, was burned alive in 1209, herded into the cathedral, which was then set on fire by the pope's soldiers. 'Kill them all. God will know his own,' was the order of Arnaud Amalric, the papal legate and Cistercian abbot.

47   A derogatory French slang term that is used to describe someone as rustic, akin to a hick in America or bumpkin in England.

48   A theme in Hôtel du Nord, the 1946 film directed by Marcel Carné. The film is set around the Canal Saint-Martin in Paris and includes the famous scene in which the star Arletty delivers the legendary line, '*Atmosphère! Atmosphère! Est-ce que j'ai une gueule d'atmosphère?*' Arletty was a remarkable actress criticised for her conduct during the occupation. Her response: '*Mon coeur est francais, mais mon cul est international.*'

49   The Molotov-Ribbentrop Pact signed on August 23, 1939 was a non-aggression treaty between Nazi Germany and the Soviet Union. It included a secret protocol that divided Eastern Europe into spheres of influence, leading to the invasion and partition of Poland in September 1939, triggering World War II.

50   If you are lucky they will give you cake.

51   Famous books and films about the Spanish Civil War (1936-1939) include *Homage to Catalonia*, George Orwell (1938); *For Whom the Bell Tolls*, Ernest Hemingway (1940) *Land and Freedom*, (1995, dir. Ken Loach).

52   Dolores Ibárruri Gómez (December 9, 1895 – November 12, 1989) was a Spanish Communist leader, born into a mining family in the Basque country. She was famous for her oratory, rallying support for the Republican cause against Franco's Nationalists. Exiled to the Soviet Union, she returned to Spain in 1977 after Franco's death.

53   Oradour-sur-Glane is a village in the Haute-Vienne department of France that became the site of a tragic massacre during World War II. On June 10, 1944, soldiers from the 2nd SS Panzer Division Das Reich killed 643 civilians, including men, women, and children, and destroyed the village.

54   Editor from 2009 to 2024.

55   Campaigners have accused BBC bosses of 'promoting the cult of gender ideology' in recent episodes when fans were introduced to Rose Noble, the transgender daughter of Donna Noble, who blasts the Doctor for 'assuming the gender' of a rat-like furry alien. In March 1984, Antiques Roadshow expert Ronnie Archer-Morgan refused to value an ivory bangle that was linked to the slave trade. In the school drama Waterloo Road its school drama Waterloo Road a trans schoolgirl visits her dying grandmother in her care home and is offended when the old woman 'deadnames' her - calling her by her former male name. The examples are endless.

56   BBC Verify, launched in 2023, is the BBC's so-called fact-checking unit dedicated to countering disinformation and providing in-depth analysis. While the exact operational costs of BBC Verify have not been publicly disclosed, they are estimated at £40 million per year. Verify has faced numerous controversies since its inception. In November 2024, it was criticized for alleged political bias in its reporting on farmer protests against proposed inheritance tax changes. The unit cited Dan Neidle, a lawyer and former Labour activist, as an independent tax expert to support government estimates, while dismissing counterclaims from the Country Land and Business Association. Critics, including former BBC staff, have questioned the necessity and effectiveness of BBC Verify. In September 2023, Marianna Spring, the BBC disinformation correspondent, faced allegations of embellishing her CV. Reports indicated that in 2018, she claimed to have worked alongside BBC correspondent Sarah Rainsford during the World Cup in Russia, a claim that was later disputed.

57   BBC former director of television Danny Cohen wrote in the *Daily Telegraph* in March 2024 that BBC News was 'plunging new depths when it comes to its reporting of the Israel-Hamas war' bringing shame on the corporation. publicly-funded organisation. The evidence of BBC partiality is overwhelming. In October 2023, an explosion occurred at the Al-Ahli Arab Hospital in Gaza City, resulting in significant casualties. Initial reports from various media outlets, including the BBC, suggested that the blast was caused by an Israeli airstrike. BBC correspondent Jon Donnison stated during live coverage that, given the explosion's magnitude, it was 'hard to see what else this could

be.' It turned out to have been a misfired Hamas missile. In February 2025 the BBC broadcast shoddy propaganda about an ordinary Palestinian boy without disclosing he was the son of a Hamas government minister. A report published in September 2024 accused the BBC of breaching its own editorial guidelines over 1,500 times during its coverage of the Israel-Hamas conflict. The report by British-Israeli lawyer Trevor Asserson was based on work by approximately 20 lawyers and 20 data scientists using artificial intelligence to analyse over nine million words from the BBC's output across various platforms, including television, radio, online news, podcasts, and social media. The findings indicated that BBC editorial guidelines had been breached more than 1,500 times - a 'deeply worrying pattern of bias against Israel' by the BBC.

[58] The domestic services also have a problem. Throughout its history, the BBC has had a problem with infiltration. Guy Burgess, a member of the infamous Cambridge Five spy ring joined the BBC's s Talks Department in 1936, leveraging his position to gather and transmit sensitive information to the Soviet Union. Burgess's activities remained undetected for years, allowing him to ascend to roles within British intelligence and the Foreign Office before his eventual defection to the Soviet Union in 1951.

[59] This has been done in France to the tune of €4 billion annually where the public broadcasters, particularly France Radio, exemplify bien-pensant thinking. Taxpayers also subsidise the press by an estimated €500 million annually through tax concessions, direct payments and other privileges such as subsidised postal rates.

[60] The BBC appears institutionally obsessed with this art. BBC Radio Manchester even featured a unique takeover by drag queens for one day. This initiative aimed to 'celebrate and highlight drag culture, providing listeners with diverse perspectives and entertainment from the drag community.'

[61] Burchill: 'The freedom that women were supposed to have found in the Sixties largely boiled down to easy contraception and abortion; things to make life easier for men, in fact.'

[62] *La Fabrication de l'information*: Editions La Dècouverte, 1999.

[63] Adam Boulton, former political editor of Sky News, argued on BBC's Newsnight in 2023 that GB News be shut down for disturbing the 'delicate and important broadcast ecology' of UK broadcasting .

[64] A Non-Crime Hate Incident is a police-recorded event where hate is 'perceived' as a motivating factor but no crime has been committed. Introduced in the UK to track potentially harmful behaviour, NCHIs can appear in background checks affecting employment.

[65] Perhaps new, new journalism. There was a previous 'new journalism' that emerged in the 1960s and 1970s, characterised by literary techniques associated with fiction. Writers like Tom Wolfe, Truman Capote, Hunter S. Thompson, and Gay Talese popularised it in magazines like *Esquire*, the *New Yorker*, and *Rolling Stone*. Then everyone did it and it was no longer new.

[66] I. F. Stone (December 24, 1907 – June 18, 1989), was an American investigative journalist, writer, and author renowned for his politically progressive views and fearless reporting. His self-published newsletter, *I. F. Stone's Weekly* (1953–1971), is ranked 16th among the top hundred works of journalism in the 20th century by New York University's journalism department. I was an avid follower. He taught me the importance of admitting when you don't know.

[67] There was an entire museum dedicated to news in Washington D.C., the Newseum. It closed in 2019 when the news industry refused to write the checks to pay for it.

[68] *Beyond Babel: New Directions in Communications*, 1972. Andre Deutsch, London; Simon & Schuster, New York.

[69] Sir Harold Evans (1928-2020) was a renowned British-American journalist and editor, best known for his tenure as editor of the *Sunday Times* (1967-1981). Evans later became editor of *The Times* but resigned due to conflicts with Rupert Murdoch. Moving to the U.S., he led the Atlantic Monthly Press and Random House.

[70] The Macmillan publishing and political dynasty also produced influential politicians, notably Harold Macmillan (1894-1986), who served as UK Prime Minister (1957-1963). Nature is currently owned by the German Springer media group.

[71] Sir John Maddox, in *What Remains to Be Discovered* (1998), explored the vast unknowns of science. While some mysteries have been partially addressed since then, many remain unresolved in physics, cosmology, medicine, the origin of life, the human brain, fusion energy and space exploration.

INDEX